A Look Back

Businesses in the Juniata Valley

On the front cover – Smith's Atlantic Service Station was located at the corner of Market and Grand Streets in Lewistown, owned and operated from the 1930s to 1951, by Cloyd C. Smith. His son, Carl Smith, tells the story on Page 57.

On the back cover – Memorabilia from the past includes useful items given to loyal customers, like this grocery list/cooking time table from the Old Port Store near Port Royal. Wayne E. Taylor tells the story on Page 129.

The Sentinel

Lewistown, Pennsylvania

Introduction

It's one thing to read written accounts of the past by historians,

It's even better to read what those who lived the history have to say.

And it's even better to see photos that help you look beyond the main subject of the pictures for the details of everyday life — what  kinds of cars were on the streets, the signs, the products on the shelves, the prices of things, what they wore, ate and smoked.

Thanks to contributions from readers, previous writers, and old books, all of these options were available to create this look back at businesses in the Juniata Valley.

My favorites are the old photos, and there are plenty in this volume. I spent a lot of time looking at everything in the photos, especially the ones showing store interiors and dressed windows. What a history story they tell!

In addition to photos and written memories of local business, a lot of people offered advertising and promotional items that tell their own tales of business long ago. Lucky for us, people save stuff — bags and boxes bearing store names, novelty items handed out to customers, useful items like matches, yardsticks and pens and much more. Some see those items as trash; others as historical records.

Print advertisements, from newspapers as well as old books, also have a story to tell and serve as an interesting look at the past, so there are plenty of those in this book, too.

Several people also lent me valuable resources that helped me verify and clarify some details about various businesses and industries. They included Pam Goss, who shared her 1894 edition of "Lewistown, Penna., As It Is;" Keith Metzger, who shared "A Survey of the Resources and Opportunities of Mifflin County, Pennsylvania," published in 1947; Rob Postal, who shared a large binder with background information about the area's major industries; Joan North, who shared a 1970 City Directory; Randy Cutshall, who shared newspapers from 1947; and Pat Kauffman, who shared newspapers from 1936.

I am grateful to the many people who had a hand in making this book possible.

Other resources used to tie the stories together in this book included: various edition of The Sentinel; "The Gem of the Juniata Valley: Lewistown, Pennsylvania," published in 1909; "Historical Souvenir of Lewistown, Penna.," published in 1925; "Souvenir Booklet on the History of Lewistown, Pennsylvania and the Greater Lewistown Area," published in 1970; the Mifflin County Historical Society, the Juniata County Historical Society and a bunch of old stuff I found in a box under my desk, fortunately left by other reporters/editors long ago.

— Jane Cannon Mort

Ruth Eddy, Publisher
Compiled by: Jane Cannon Mort
 Special Projects Editor
Photo editor: Buffie Boyer
Cover design: Jennifer Knepp

Library of Congress Catalog-in-Publication Data
A Look Back

ISBN 978-0-9830846-6-2

Table of Contents

Mifflin County

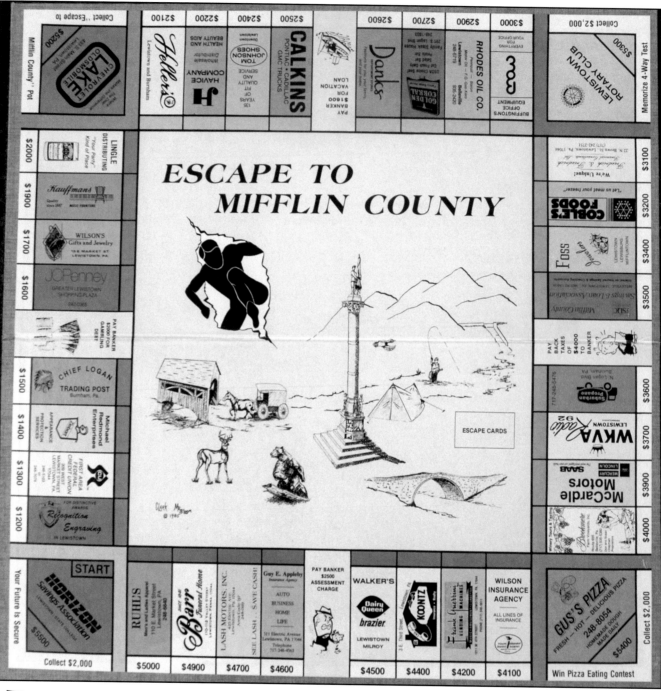

The limited edition "Escape to Mifflin County" board game, based on the popular "Monopoly" game, was published in 1985 as a fundraiser for the Rotary Club of Lewistown. The play money and escape cards also featured ads from a variety of local businesses, industries and organizations.

Submitted by Bob McCombie
Rotary Club of Lewistown

4

Remembering:

Downtown Lewistown in the 1940s and '50s

Photos submitted by Carole Campbell

Gift box from Danks

By Carole A. Campbell
Lewistown

Downtown Lewistown was the place to be, especially on Saturdays, when I was growing up.

There were lots of stores, restaurants and movie theaters. The Senior Group I have often take memory trips through the town remembering what used to be, and wishing it was like that now. It is fun to see who remembers what places, and what places they come up with that some us of don't even know about.

My first job was in Murphy's Five and Ten. I made 50 cents an hour and worked at the candy counter. What a temptation — wanting to taste some of the fresh candy as we filled the bins. It was especially fun at Easter, when my friend, Helen Staronka, and I got extra hours after school to decorate the eggs and other candies in a special area downstairs. "Gossy," we called her, was in charge of the candy counter, and the floor lady in charge of our area was Helen Weaver. Another reason I like working at the candy counter was that it was close to the music counter, so I could hear all the newest hit records as they played them to attract buyers.

Living at 5 North Grand Street, Lewistown, made a walk to downtown Lewistown not too far.

My memories started right around the corner, on Market Street, at the Spa Restaurant, where I spent many hours drinking vanilla Cokes, eating Hartley's potato chips dipped in ketchup, and talking with my friends, plus the Arseniu sisters, who worked there for their father,

owner of the restaurant.

The restaurant was originally located in a small, narrow building beside what used to be Wolf's Furniture Store, about a half block down on the other side of Market Street, and was one of the many places to get hot dogs in a two block area.

Mentioning Wolf's brought to mind going there on Saturday nights when they have some kind of sale and gave away prizes. I remember one time winning ice cube trays. I think that was an unusual pastime for a young girl.

On to the next block. The first store I remember was Quigleys, where I would buy Smith Brothers licorice cough drops, Sen-Sens and other little things. Still have a very, very small doll from a box of them that I fell in love with and bought.

Up the street a little way was Bunkers, where I purchased my first Scrabble game, which I still have. Now it sits on the shelf in my basement, and I play Scrabble on my phone with several friends. Miss the many times playing with my friend, Mary Hughes, in the summer afternoons while we ate Hartley's chips and drank Cokes.

Now, that reminds me of the two of us stopping at Headings drugstore on the square for chocolate ice cream sodas, and almost weekly going to Laskaris for hot dogs before going to the movies, mostly at the Rialto, and sometimes the Embassy. We could have gone to the Pastime for free since her father had an office above the

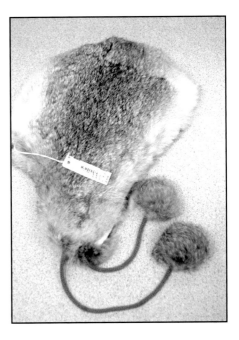

Chinchilla hat, complete with tag, from McMeen's

Photo submitted by Susan and Carl King, Lewistown

Lewistown in the '40s and '50s

theater, but we weren't much into westerns.

On the first block of East Market Street, I remember shopping at Murphy's, McCrory's, the Famous, Goldman's and Wian's.

The second block, it was the Princess Shop and Ruhl's, where they had special sales of buying one pair of shoes and getting another for $1.

Next there was McMeen's, where I remember the money runners overhead that carried tubes with your payment to the office, and going upstairs to see Santa.

Most of the five and tens had lunch counters, but the one I remember most is the one at Rea & Derrick's.

I must back up to the square area, as I got lost with my girlfriend and the places we stopped. Must mention the Quick Lunch, where, if I remember right, you could see the hot dogs cooking on the grill right inside the window.

Did some shopping in Montgomery Wards, and remember a special dress I bought there when I was in my late teens that my future boyfriend found very attractive.

Also, on the opposite side of the square, there was a little shop beside Murphy's called Hoffman's, where I used to buy comic books. "Archie" was my favorite, and I regret not having kept all of them, as I am very nostalgic.

Back up the McMeen's, which had two stores, as did Danks, which is the store I miss most. My aunt and I shopped there a lot, even when I moved back to town after being gone for 15 years.

At Five Points was another Headings Drugstore, where we also got chocolate ice cream sodas. They had quite an array of things to buy.

Around the corner from there was Marks, where my grandmother bought all her hats. In those days, a lot of ladies and young girls wore hats to church, and my grandmother was one of them. I took up the habit in my

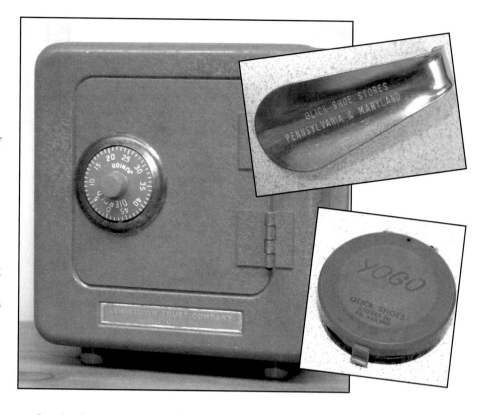

Carole Campbell's collection of memorabilia from downtown Lewistown includes mini safe from Lewistown Trust Company, a shoehorn and puzzle from Glick's Shoes.

later teenage years, but gave it up when I was in my 30s.

There were several banks, and the one I remember most was the Lewistown Trust, because it was my bank growing up. I started a Christmas club there as soon as I went to work. Russell became our bank when we returned to Lewistown in 1970. Of course, I will never forget the corner clock by the First National Bank, and I still miss it today.

That completes my tour of downtown Lewistown as I remember it when I was growing up, except for an office around the corner from Danks on Dorcas Street, where my dad took me for some paperwork I needed to get married.

After becoming a Mrs., I moved to Harrisburg with my Mr., who entered the ministry, which meant we moved to different areas where he pastored

churches within a conference that moved you a lot.

After leaving the conference, we moved back to the Lewistown area, where he continued to pastor locally. Much had changed, but still in Lewistown were some of my favorites like Danks, Murphy's, the Embassy and Laskaris.

Headings had been replaced with the first OIP, the Famous had been replaced by Glick's Shoe Store, which became my new favorite, and the Hello Shop had moved in by Russell Bank.

Now all that remains is Laskaris and the Embassy, but neither are the same as I remember them being in the good, old days.

In conclusion, I will just say that I thoroughly enjoyed the old downtown Lewistown, and it was a wonderful place to me as a child and teenager.

Postcards from the past

Postcards from the collection of Nancy Peachey showing downtown Lewistown originally appeared in "I Remember When ... II," a special section published by The Sentinel in 2009.

East Market Street, postmarked 1909

West Market Street

Monument Square, postmarked 1966

Monument Square

The Iron Front Store

The front and back of a calendar card in the collection of Chris Kearns, of Lewistown, advertises Goodhart & Houtz Iron Front Store in Lewistown. The calendar is dated 1884.

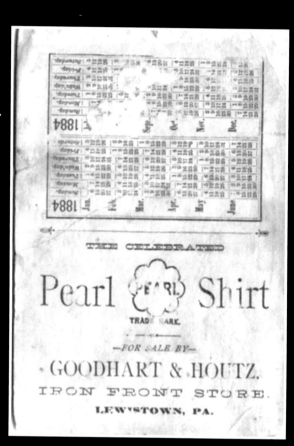

A Front View

Of this Store gives but a faint idea of its extent and the immense stock on hand. In addition to the large and completely filled store room there is

A Large Warehouse

at the rear with two extensive floors packed with Toys, Games, Express Wagons and Tricycles.

Confectioneries,

Fruits and Toys

are the leaders here, and this store is the leader in the business. You can get anything you want and I can help you solve the problem of selecting holiday, birthday and other gifts.

Schools, Sunday Schools and Stores Supplied at Wholesale Prices.

D. GROVE,

16 East Market Street. Lewistown, Pa.

Iron Front Store.

The Oldest and Most Reliable Store in Lewistown. It has been in successful operation for 25 years, and to-day it stands in the very front rank of all others.

At this store you can always find the largest and best stock of

An advertisement for the same store appears in the 1894 book, "Lewistown, Penna., As It Is," by H. J. Fosnot, of the Sentinel and Democrat, reprinted here courtesy of Pam Goss, of Lewistown.

The bottom part of the ad, under the heading "Iron Front Store," describes the business:

"The oldest and most reliable store in Lewistown. It has been in successful operation for 25 years and today it stands in the very front rank of all others."

"At this store you can always find the largest and best stock of DRESS GOODS of all kinds, from the cheaper grades to the finest novelties in Silks the market affords. Our NOTION DEPARTMENT is always up to date, in Kid and all other kinds of gloves, hosiery, underwear, etc.

"Politeness, attention and kindness are always used in serving the patrons of this store. We do not importune any person to buy."

— John C. Houtz

Muthersbaugh's Drugstore

Submitted by Mary Berrier Hughes, Lewistown

This photo of Muthersbaugh's Drugstore in Lewistown appeared in the 2013 calendar published by the Mifflin County Historical Society. The original photograph was donated by Mary Berrier Hughes to the historical society. The caption on the calendar states:

Muthersbaugh's Drugstore, 1900 — J.A. Muthersbaugh was engaged in the drug business for about 52 years, 37 years in Lewistown, where this large drugstore was located. He graduated from the Philadelphia College of Pharmacy, July 7, 1874. He worked 10 years in Philadelphia, then opened a drugstore in Harrisburg for one year before coming to Lewistown, where he located his store at 110 East Market Street, Lewistown.

In the photo, the man on the right is Hughes' great-uncle, Jacob Muthersbaugh, and the woman in the center aisle is Caroline Muthersbaugh, his sister.

Store's lights still on

By Shirley Miller
Lewistown

In 1941, our former pastor, Victor Hahn, of Lake Park United Methodist Church at the corner of West Fourth Street and Crystal Springs Avenue, Lewistown, found out that F.W. Woolworth 5&10 store on Market Street was doing some re-modeling and was installing new lighting. Rev. Hahn checked to see what they were doing with the old fixtures. He obtained them free of charge and we are still using them in our sanctuary.

They are still very special to us and we also have memories of downtown Lewistown when we see them in our church.

Photo submitted by Wayne Taylor

Woolworth's, Market Street, Lewistown

9

Eateries

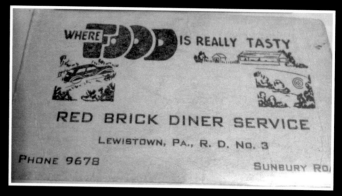

Barbara Cooper, of Burnham. found this card from the Red Brick Diner Service among old pictures that her family saved, but she does not have any information about the business.

Patsy Carson, of Belleville, doesn't remember the name of the restaurant in the pictures above and below, but she does know that it was owned by Cletus and Dorothy Eddinger, her parents. Co-owners were Patsy's aunt and uncle, James and Mary Hartman. The business was located on U.S. Highway 522, just west of Lewistown, approximately where Snappy's Convenience Store is located today.

This holiday card from the J. R. Swartz Fancy Bakery and Confectionery, Lewistown, is from the collection of Chris Kearns, of Lewistown.

Banks

Lewistown Trust Co. Building, Lewistown, Pa.

A snapshot in time — October 1, 1945, to be exact — is made possible by purusing the pages of a hardback book called "A Survey of the Resources and Opportunities of Mifflin County, Pennsylvania." It was published by the Chamber of Commerce Mifflin County's Development Committee on March 15, 1947, and lists, among a great deal of other information, all of the banking institutions in the county at that time:

• First National Bank of Lewistown, 33 East Market Street, Lewistown
  • Kishacoquillas Valley National Bank, Belleville
  • Lewistown Trust Company, 102 East Market Street, Lewistown
  • McVeytown National Bank, McVeytown
  • Milroy Banking Company, Milroy
  • Reedsville National Bank, Reedsville
  • Russell National Bank, 32 East Market Street, Lewistown.

The book is owned by Keith Metzger, of Belleville, a former employee of the old First National Bank of Lewistown, which is no more.

Postcards in the collection of Chris Kearns, of Lewistown, show the Lewistown Trust Company building a the corner of Market and Brown streets in Lewistown. The postcard above is circa 1917.

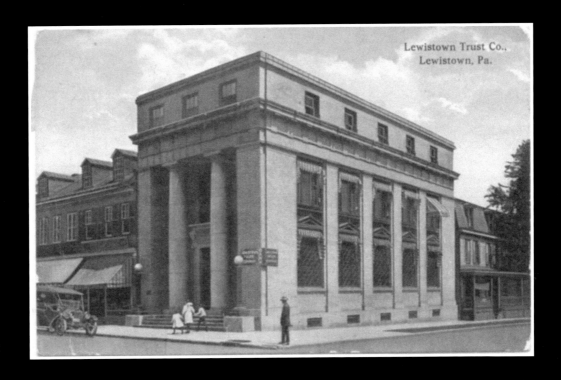

Lewistown Trust Co., Lewistown, Pa.

Hotels

Marge Searer, of Lewistown, found this undated postcard of the Green Gables in her attic. It originally appeared in "I Remember When ... II," a special section published by The Sentinel in 2009. The imprint on the back of the card explains that the "privately-owned small hotel is situated at the foot-hills of Jack's Mountain along the Juniata River running through the famous Lewistown Narrows." The hotel had been built around a "century old" barn, with all entrances remaining the same. The lobby and dining room were the stables, and the timbers remained in their original positions. The stairway of the hotel had once been the "hay-hole," and the second floor, the loft. The lounge facing the garden "was the over-shot of the barn, and the lily pond the watering trough."

Submitted by Marge Searer, Lewistown

HOTEL LEWISTOWN
LEWISTOWN PA.
ERECTED 1937

HOTEL HUNTINGDON
HUNTINGDON PA.
UNDER SAME MANAGEMENT

Submitted by Wayne Taylor, Mifflintown

Hotel Lewistown, 1940s

HOTEL LEWISTOWN
LEWISTOWN, PA.
The Stop that Starts your Smiles

Submitted by Chris Kearns, Lewistown

The COLEMAN Hotel
LEWISTOWN, PENNSYLVANIA

Submitted by Chris Kearns, Lewistown

The Coleman Hotel

Joe Katz Store

Photo3 submitted by Margie Zavacky

Margie Zavacky, of Yeagertown, worked at Joe Katz men's clothing store in downtown Lewistown for 14 years as a secretary/Girl Friday. Photos from her collection include a shot of the building in March 1970, as it looked before it was torn down for redevelopment, and the grand opening of the new Joe Katz store at the corner of Market and Brown streets in Lewistown during the redevelopment in the 1970s. Pictured at the ribbon cutting ceremony are Mary Ann Katz, Bill Katz, Mrs. Katz and Mayor John Lawler.

1909

TWENTY ONE YEARS

OF

FAITHFUL SERVICE

AND

HONEST VALUES

IN

CLOTHING & FURNISHINGS

FOR

THE COLLEGIATE BOY

OR

THE CONSERVATIVE MAN

JOE KATZ, INC.

1925 advertisement

1923 to 1984 — 61 years in Lewistown

Photo by Kepler

A brief history of The Kepler Studio

By Forest K. Fisher, of Reedsville, grandson of the founder

The Kepler Studio, a six-decade Lewistown business, was founded by photographer Luther Forest Kepler Sr. (1902-1969) in 1923. His interest in photography began as early as 1910 when he took snapshots holding a small box camera. The studio he founded remained in downtown Lewistown until 1984.

Kepler's career as a master of the photographic arts and sciences was to see him capture on still and motion picture film, everything from the governors of Pennsylvania and the King of England to Canadian moose and the ravens of Alan Seeger State Park. He, along with his brother James, photographed hundreds of weddings, special community events, local industries and literally thousands of school students along the way.

Starting at the end of the silent era of motion pictures, Luther was also an accomplished cinematographer. He worked with a Hollywood director in the late 1920s, filming local theatrical productions, U.S. Army war training films during World War II, highway safety and documentaries for the Commonwealth of Pennsylvania in the '40s and '50s, and productions on life in the outdoors and hunting.

Luther also operated the once popular Mifflin County tourist attraction, Alexander Caverns, located in Armagh Township, for the 13 years prior to this show cave's permanent commercial closing in 1953.

His brother and future partner, James Arthur Kepler (1906-1991),

Luther F. Kepler Sr. inspects a 35mm Leica camera at the 1937 Mifflin County Fair. The Leica was an innovative camera of the era, with variable lenses and easily processed roll film.

Photo submitted by Forest Fisher

also had an early introduction to picture taking, when he discovered a small camera in a box of Cracker Jack, according to a story he told years later.

James's career included Civil Defense Director of Mifflin County during World War II, a run for the state legislature in the 1960s, and Civil Defense Director Coordinator in the 1970s and '80s, marked by the Flood of 1972.

The naming of the Kepler Bridge, over Jack's Creek, is recognition by the county commissioners at the time for his work during and after that flood. He also worked closely with local fire companies as emergency management coordinator.

While working as a photographer, he traveled throughout New England, photographing knitting mills, and to Cleveland, Ohio, to photograph the General Electric works.

Both men spent a lifetime dedicated to the art and science of photography, being the first studio in Mifflin County to process and produce prints from natural color photographic film.

The story of The Kepler Studio begins with Luther in 1923. His search for making a living as a photographer was one of distance, geography and pure chance. After attending Lewistown High School until 1918, he graduated in 1919 from Mount Hermon School for Boys, a preparatory school located near Northfield, Massachusetts. Luther completed the business course at Susquehanna University in 1920, never really expecting a career in photography. Luther's father, George B. M. Kepler, was a lifelong banker, helping establish banks in Blairs Mills, Pennsylvania, Kitzmiller, West Virginia, and Mount Union and at this time, was assistant cashier at the Mifflin County National Bank. Luther's older brother, Irvin T. Kepler, likewise made a career in banking in Pennsylvania and Maryland. It was expected Luther might follow in this direction as well.

When the Susquehanna University experience ended, only odd jobs were in the offing. Luther worked at a dye

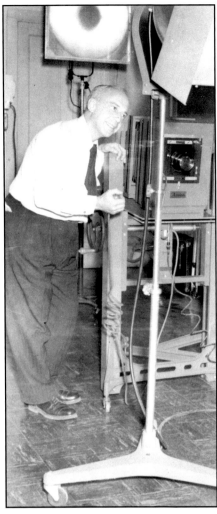

Photos submitted by Forest Fisher

James A. "Jimmie" Kepler in the Kepler Studio camera room at 28 East Market Street. Jimmie is shown with the full-sized studio camera and new strobe lights acquired by the business in the late 1950s.

factory in Lancaster County, was an armed guard for the U.S. Mail for three months at the Paradise, Pennsylvania, post office, where he met his future wife, and even picked apples with his future father-in-law.

The venture into commercial and portrait photography began in Harrisburg in 1921, while working part-time for the J. W. Roshon Studio of that city. During the winter and spring of 1922, Luther was sent by Roshon to Hersheypark. There, he managed a small studio next to the park's carousel, making souvenir photographs for Hersheypark visitors. Business boomed, and he took on a helper

Luther F. Kepler, Sr. in Kepler Studio camera room at 28 East Market Street, 1961. The Polaroid camera on the mantel was then in use to make preliminary black/white shots before a subject was photographed in color.

named Gardner in the summer of 1922. They supplemented the photo business by selling hedge trimmers on the side along the street of Hershey and nearby communities.

Taking a real interest in the art of photography, Luther left the Hersheypark job, and traveled a circuit to McKeesport, Reading, and York making baby portraits for Roshon. While at the Harrisburg Roshon studio, he photographed Mr. and Mrs. Gifford Pinchot during Pinchot's first term as Pennsylvania governor, and worked in Lewistown on a part-time basis for local photographers Gibbs & Healy.

During the period 1921-1923, he became acquainted with photographers Ed Gutshall and Charlie Sands, owners of a studio in Old Orchard, Maine, and another studio in Harrisburg. In early 1923, Luther left Roshon's and managed the Sands Studio in Harrisburg until later that year.

Luther got word that the studio in Old Orchard would be closing. He bought the stock and equipment of

Photos submitted by Forest Fisher

Exterior of 127 East Market Street (when the BonTon store is today). This was the second location for the studio, including the studio and gift shop at street level and the Kepler apartments above. Luther F. Kepler Sr. and wife Iva Kemrer, lived here with children Iva Anne and Luther Jr., along with Luther Sr.'s mother, Anne Elizabeth Kelper.

Gutshall and Sands in Maine. This was accomplished in the summer of 1923 and became the basis of The Kepler Studio's initial photographic equipment - enlargers, print dryers, developing trays and tanks and a supply of chemicals. With the urging and support of future wife Iva Kemrer, he decided to open his own studio in Lewistown, specializing in commercial and portrait photography, choosing a location at 35 Chestnut Street.

The Kepler Studio opened for business at 35 Chestnut Street. Then quickly moved into larger quarters at 127 East Market Street, where the Bon Ton store is today, on Thanksgiving weekend, 1923, in recently vacated and renovated rooms over the G. C. Murphy 5 & 10 Cent Store. This establishment was a portrait studio and gift shop. First photographs made in The Kepler Studio were of Anne Elizabeth Kepler, mother of Luther and James. The first family sitting in the studio was of Mr. and Mrs. J. Foster Sankey and daughter, Mary Margaret, of Reedsville.

Eventually Murphy's moved to another location on Market Street and the studio expanded downstairs around 1926. The family lived in apartments above and the gift shop became more extensive below, selling everything from greeting cards to chocolates made

This window of 127 East Market Street was on the west side of building.

Interior of 127 East Market Street gift shop featured an extensive line of cards, gifts and even candies available for shoppers, in addition to the full line of photographic service.

by Lewistown confectioner Adam Dughi, and even antiques.

In 1932-33, the studio was moved to 25 E. Market Street, on the ground floor. At this time, the family was living in Paradise, Pennsylvania, part-time, to help with Luther's in-laws, who ran the Paradise Lodge. Then in 1935, another move, to 28 E. Market Street, next to the Russell National Bank. The studio relocated to 28 N. Dorcas Street and remained until the late '60s, following the demolition of the Y.M.C.A. on Dorcas Street and subsequent redevelopment of that block.

The Kepler Studio's final move was to the corner of Third and Dorcas streets. Address: 201 E. Third. Here it remained until its closing February 1,

1984. The photographic studio had a business life of 61 years.

It was always surprising, even though the Depression years hit Mifflin County as hard as anywhere, there was a steady market for photographs of the new baby, a wedding, special anniversary or uniquely shaped vegetable from the garden.

The Kepler Studio usually had a partner for most of its existence. The first was Ellis K. LeCrone, who ran the gift shop portion of the business from 1926 to 1928. The partnership existed until it was dissolved by mutual agreement April 1, 1928. Prior to this date, Luther's brother, James A. Kepler, had worked at Lewistown Trust Company, but an offer from Luther to become a partner brought

James into the business that April. Luther was involved in filming a silent movie at the time.

During the spring of 1928, Luther was hired as the chief cinematographer on the set of movie-maker and director, Salvado P. B. Cudia, who shot a silent film in the Huntingdon-Lock Haven-Clearfield-Philipsburg area and later in Lewistown. Embassy Theatre owner Harold D. Cohen was a guest on the set during the filming. Such promotional movies used local actors and extras for the production. The papers advertised "Hollywood brought to ..." and the name of your town was inserted, along with the theatre where you could "See How the Movies Are Made — Cameras, Directors, Lights, Etc." A fire scene was filmed in Philipsburg, at noon April 12, 1928, with the hero and heroine. A car driven by the villain went careening over a high cliff near Lock Haven, all part of the local film. Accounts of the production were recorded in the Philipsburg newspaper.

James managed the studio in the late 1930s and early 1940s, while Luther worked for the Pennsylvania Department of Highways Photographic Unit. He was chief photographer for the highways department from 1939 to 1942. In 1942, Luther, as a cinematographer, began making military training films at Penn State College for the War Department. He returned to the studio full time after 1945.

Luther also was among the photographers who photographed King George VI and Queen Elizabeth in Ottawa, Canada, during their royal tour in 1939. Having participated in and filmed moose hunts in nearby Quebec, flying from Lewistown to Canada was an easy flight with friend and county flying ace Jack Kratzer.

Briefly, in the 1950s and early 1960s, the Kepler brothers operated a branch studio in State College, making primarily portrait work for fraternities and sororities, and individuals at the university.

Photographs for postcards became quite a business. Thousands were produced over the years. In 1962, the processing of color film was done on the premises, a first for a central Pennsylvania studio.

Luther and James remained partners until Luther's sudden death January 6, 1969. James continued the commercial and portrait photographic business until his retirement February 1, 1984. He died after a lengthy illness, February 17, 1991.

High school seniors and other yearbook photographs were taken by the Kepler Studio of all Mifflin County high schools at one time, countless weddings and family portraits, sporting events, parades, state and national dignitaries, you name it, the Kepler brothers photographed it.

In more than six decades of business, the Kepler Studio recorded a large swath of the life and times of Lewistown and greater Mifflin County. It was an honor to have your treasured picture signed, "Photo by Kepler."

Photo and clippings submitted by Forest Fisher

Kepler Studio at 28 North Dorcas Street, January 1969, beside the former Lewistown YMCA

OPENS NEW STUDIO

The Kepler Studio, 127 East Market Street, which opened for business on Saturday is one of the most attractive business places in this section, the rooms over the C. G. Murphy 5 & 10 Cent Store being entirely renovated prior to the opening of the new establishment, which is being conducted by Luther Kepler.

Previous to coming to his home here to open an up to date photography establishment, with all metropolitan equipment, Mr. Kepler conducted a like business at Old Orchard, Maine, going there from Roshon's Studio in Harrisburg. During his stay with the capital photographer and artist, Mr. Kepler photographed Governor and Mrs. Pinchot, making the prints which were used in many of the metropolitan newspapers after Mr. Pinchot's election.

The new studio has the very latest equipment, including an Eastman camera that reproduces an 8x10 picture, which can be enlarged to any size.

In the reception room, which is 17x 15 feet in size, tan and blue form the color scheme, making a very attractive appearance.

Clipping from the Sentinel noting the Kepler Studio opening in 1923.

1932 Lewistown Street Directory ad

Kepler Studio Moves Business

Kepler Studio, which has been engaged in commercial and portrait photography in Lewistown nearly 40 years, has moved to a new location. The studio began operations at 28 N. Dorcas St. last week.

Not only does the new location provide more space for studio and darkroom facilities, but is also located so to allow ample parking space for visitors.

This is the fourth move for the studio since its beginning in Lewistown in 1923. Each time it has moved, better facilities have been initiated for the customer.

Luther F. Kepler opened the first site at 127 E. Market St. in 1923. The first establishment was a portrait studio - gift shop combination. In 1933 it was moved to 25 E. Market St. and in 1935 to 28 E. Market St.

Mr. Kepler's brother joined him after the original founding. Mrs. Luther F. Kepler also works in the studio and their daughter, Mrs. Ann (Kepler) Fisher does oil portrait work.

The studio was established primarily for portrait work, but also does commercial work. The Keplers recently entered the field of natural color photography.

"I have experienced a tremendous transition in the field of photography in the last ten years, especially in the techniques of black and white and natural color," Luther Kepler said.

Kepler's Studio is the oldest photographic establishment still in business in Lewistown.

Clipping from The Sentinel, early 1960s, about the change of location to North Dorcas Street.

'Photo by Kepler'

Photos Win Prizes in 'Pro' Contest

D. DUGHI

Kepler Photos—Sentinel Engraving
CONNIE SADLER

First photographic sitting at the Kepler Studio in 1923, believed to be at the 35 Chestnut Street location, captured Anne Elizabeth Kepler and son James A. Kepler. Portrait taken by Luther F. Kepler Sr.

Clippings from the 1930s reporting on awards received by the Kepler Studio at a professional photography exhibit in New York state.

Submitted by Forest Fisher

GOLD RIBBONS FOR PORTRAITS

Kepler Studio Receives Awards at Binghamton, N. Y., Convention

Six photographs, three commercial and three portrait pictures, were entered in the 31st annual convention of the Professional Photographic Society of New York held at Binghamton, N. Y., April 12 and 13, by Kepler Studio, 25 East Market Street.

All six were accepted by the society for display and each one was awarded a gold ribbon as being outstanding in its class. The exhibits were returned to the studio here several days ago and have been placed on display.

In the portrait class were three photographic etchings which the Kepler brothers believe to be the finest examples of their work in all their years experience. The one was an etching of D. Dughi, 5 East Market Street; another was an etching of Stetson Kieferle, 19 North Pine Street, in the act of tuning a violin. Both photographs were taken several years ago. The third was an etching of Connie Sadler, young daughter of Mr. and Mrs. J. O. Sadler of Milroy. It was taken about Christmastime last year. With the portraits finished as etchings, the three commercial subjects were done as bromoils and made of "Dottie" an English Pointer, "Princess Patsy," a Cocker Spaniel; and "Hypo" a collie. All three dogs were owned by Luther Kepler and registered with the American Kennel Club.

Two of the three prize-winning exhibits are shown here of D. Dughi and Connie Sadler. The pictures are from the original negative from which the etchings were made.

Photographs in the Kepler Studio street window display featuring Lance Ufema and Mary Kathryn Snook in 1948. Photo courtesy of Julie Ufema.

19

Growing up at 'The Diana'

By Deb Runk
Lewistown

Growing up in Lewistown, I remember the one place I enjoyed hanging out was a small place right around the square called "The Diana." They had the best hoagies in Lewistown.

It opened in 1930, and in 1947, a couple, Pete and Carolyn Marinos bought it.

I was 14 years old when I started hanging out, after I got out of school. Sometimes I would stay there until 4 p.m., which at that time I had to be home for supper.

It was a small place, but there was a lot of love and kindness in those walls.

Amanda Karakantas also worked there. She was Pete's sister, and she was a beautiful woman. I took to her right away, and over the next few years she became a second mother to me.

Pete and Carolyn ran a family business, and they were respected by all. They also ran a candy shop that sold chocolates, a place where many bought their Easter candy. They had three children, John, Steve (who since

Photo submitted by Deb Runk
The Diana, Market Street, Lewistown

has passed away) and Tina.

Good times were hanging out, playing the jukebox and talking to Amanda when she was on her breaks. As long as we were quiet and respect-ful, we were allowed to stay.

My mother was a good woman, but like many teens, I couldn't talk to her. So Amanda became my second mother, one who kept me on the straight and narrow.

In 1970, I left the area. I was out of Lewistown for 17 years. Over that time, I would visit and stay for a couple weeks or so. Every time I was in town, the first place I would go was the Diana.

Pete, Carolyn and Amanda always greeted me with open arms, and Amanda was always interested in what was happening in my life. They were such caring people which, in turn, made their eatery a place with delicious food, and a place with true heart.

Pete and Carolyn have since passed away. Amanda left the area to live near her son, Paul, and his family.

Whenever I think back about those times, I think about how this wonderful family shaped a lot of my life, all for the better. I have a lot of appreciation and respect for Amanda, who always had time for me. I truly love her with all my heart. I also loved those super good hoagies, none other have ever been as good as theirs.

Shopping in downtown Lewistown

Merchandise bags, gift boxes are now keepsakes

Gene Hughes, of Lewistown, has a bag from Marrone's.

Leona Shellenberger, of Mifflintown, has a black gift box from Ruhl's.

Gene Hughes also has a bag from Mussettia's.

Goss Candies

Display Room   Office   Cook Room

H. B. GOSS

317 Valley St.

MANUFACTURER OF

High Grade Fork Dipped

CHOCOLATES

This industry was started in 1913, at the corner of Logan and Spruce Streets, with the maximum capacity of a few pounds per day. Since that time the fame of our products has grown enormously and spread far and wide. In 1921 the plant was moved to its present location, extra modern machinery installed, and capacity enlarged to several tons of the best of sweets per day.

As evidence of our superior quality, our largest buyer is, and has been, our local jobber, S. Will Shunkwiler.

1925 advertisement

The Goss Candies sign is a part of the collection of old signs and photos owned by Frank and Kirk Stevens and displayed at Steven Auctioneering on Market Street in Lewistown. See more of their collection on Pages 23-25.

Goss Candies boxes from different eras are among the collections of Chris Kearns, of Lewistown, left and below, and Jane Mort, of Mifflintown.

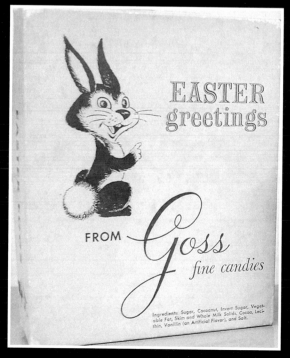

The Stevens collection

Old business signs, posters and photos owned by Frank and Kirk Stevens are on display at Stevens Auctioneering, Market Street, Lewistown.

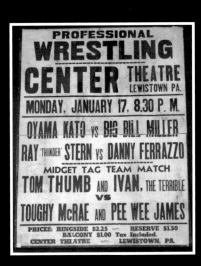

Stevens collection

BOLLINGER ESSO SERVICE

Ulsh-Shinkel Hardware

C. A. P. Ulsh   W. H. Shinkel

One of the largest and most modern hardware stores in Central Penna., enjoying large patronage in Lewistown and the surrounding territory, for which we want to express our thanks to all.

"Everything in Hardware"

Ulsh-Shinkel Hardware Co.

50-52 Valley St.

BOTH PHONES   LEWISTOWN

The Ulsh-Shinkel Hardware Co., was located on Valley Street for many years, as indicated in the advertisement above, published in 1925. The safe from the store, right, is displayed at Stevens Auctioneering, in Lewistown, owned by Frank and Kirk Stevens.

Going 'downtown' in the 1960s

Editor's note: This article originally appeared in "I Remember When ... II," a special section published by The Sentinel in 2009.

By Patricia A. (Goss) Fleck
Lewistown

Growing up within walking distance of Market Street (Shaw Avenue), I remember many of the numerous businesses that lined the streets in the early '60s. Often on Sunday evenings, my parents and I would walk "Downtown" to window shop.

Clothing stores with large windows would display the current fashions and included Danks and Co. (with two separate store front entrances), McMeen's, Montgomery Ward and the Diana Shop.

Smaller stores included The Princess Shop, The Artley, Ladies' Bazaar (on the exterior wall outside this shop, remains today an intact tile with the store name — can you find it?), Krentzman's and Goldman's. For men, specialty shops included Bob Davis, Ruhl's Clothing and Joe Katz.

Market Street proudly featured at least four furniture stores, with Penn Furniture, Kauffman's Music and Furniture, Bowman's and Wolf's. Shoe stores included Tom Johnson, Glick's, Raub and Wian's Shoes.

I remember the Franciscus Hardware Store, with its name in multicolored letters on the front of the building. There was also Clark's Hardware, Joe The Motorist's Friend and Miller's.

"Five and dimes" included Woolworth's, with its wooden floors and large ceiling fans, McCrory's and Murphy's.

Headings, Peoples and Rea and Derick drug stores all had lunch counters (as well as McCrory's and Murphy's).

Other restaurants/luncheonettes I remember include Campbell's Bar and Grill, Stafford's, and Dutch's Diner on South Brown Street.

The "banking corner" consisted of First National, with its beautiful old

G.C. Murphy Company on Monument Square was once a popular 5&10-cent store.

clock, Russell Bank and Lewistown Trust Co., with its massive concrete columns.

Goss Candies had appealing displays to tempt this future chocoholic.

But the best store ever (to a 5- to 6-year-old, at least) was Berney's Toyland!

Other memories include trips to the library on South Brown Street. Once I learned to read (which I still love to do), I looked forward to picking out books to borrow and getting new ones when they were returned.

My mother always enjoyed sewing and was very good at it, making all of my dresses, as well as her own. Danks and Co. had a large selection of material and fabrics in the lower level of the store. I remember sitting on the stools at the pattern books near the stairs and watching the feet of people passing by on the sidewalks outside!

We moved from Shaw Avenue to another area of Lewistown in 1968, but where did I go for my first job? "Downtown," of course!

While in high school, I was hired in 1971 as a clerk at Rea and Derick. It was during the Market Street renovations and the "new" R&D was not quite completed. The drugstore was temporarily located in a tiny store up the street. I remember helping move into the new store and the excitement of the grand opening.

I worked at R&D a few evenings and weekends throughout my high school years. Market Street had changed considerably from my childhood, but it still could be a very busy and bustling place.

To this day, I miss seeing the many people who would do their Christmas shopping there the last weeks of December. Or the crowds that would fill the streets during Sidewalk Sale Days in July.

Remember Green Stamps? R&D was a participating merchant in providing these stamps on purchases. Occasionally there would be promoted sale days offering double stamps. Boy, we would be busy then!

Taking store inventory was certainly different back then compared to how stores do it today. I don't remember how often it was done, but it was at least annually. Inventory Day was set and everything in the store had to be counted on that day, recording everything on paper, by hand.

I don't remember the price of very many items that I sold in 1971 working the checkout, but I do remember that cigarettes were 47 cents a pack.

On Saturdays, if I worked hours that entitled a lunch break, Campbell's Diner had the best pizzaburgers, and great hoagies were available at the Chestnut Street Superette.

Although my parents encouraged me to save some of my earnings to a savings account, I remember feeling proud that I could purchase some clothing or other items that I really wanted, for myself. My favorite clothing store was The Diana and I loved the variety of McCrory's and Murphy's, where each week I could always find my favorite Top Ten 45 records!

At Christmas, I would buy my dad's favorite brand of golf balls at Rubin's Sport Shop, and when I was a Chief Logan junior, I proudly ordered my class ring at the Royal Jewel Box.

Sadly, Market Street is far different today and shopping choices very limited. Large malls and internet sales are now the preferred choice to provide consumer's needs. Although many of the old wooden, brick and stone buildings and their businesses are gone, my memories of those days are not. I will always remember the fun during my childhood and teenage years, of going "Downtown."

Sentinel archives

Submitted by Jane Mort

McClure's jewelers was located on Valley Street, while the Bumble Bee was on Market Street in downtown Lewistown.

Window shopping

Photos courtesy of the Mifflin County Historical Society

Many people have memories of shopping at the E.E. McMeen Department Store, now The Bon Ton, on Market Street in downtown Lewistown. Enjoy window shopping on this page and the next four pages.

Window shopping at McMeen's Department Store

Window shopping at McMeen's Department Store

Window shopping at McMeen's Department Store

Window shopping at McMeen's Department Store

Sentinel archives

Market Street, Lewistown

Taking a tour through town

Editor's note: These memories submitted by readers originally appeared in "Juniata Valley 2009: I Remember When," or "I Remember When ... II," special sections published by The Sentinel in 2009.

By Lois Miller
Lewistown

In memory of Virginia Allen

This was written by my sister, Virginia Allen, who passed away five years ago.

Down Memory Lane

Do you remember when ... it was really safe the walk the streets in Lewistown, and our families would sit on the front porches on warm summer evenings?

When Lewistown had three theaters, the Embassy, Rialto and the Pastime? Matinees were 15 cents and only a nickel at the Roxy? Mr. Berney would let you sit through as many shows as you wanted.

When Murphy's had a side entrance on Main Street?

Watching the change boxes racing around the ceilings at McMeen's and Danks?

When all the stores were occupied on Market Street? Lewistown was the center of activity for all Mifflin and Juniata counties?

How about the bus service all over town, plus being able to get a transfer to any local area?

Our town clock standing at the corner of Market and Brown streets; how impressive the old Trust Company Bank was?

Wasn't it great to have a YMCA that you could walk to, the mixed swims on Friday nights?

Do you recall walking to the Lewistown Hotel to board the old K.V. train to go to the annual picnic at Kish Park?

When Kish Park was a fun place to go in the summer?

Speaking of K.V., did you ever get a popsicle stick marked "free?"

Going to a malt shop like Henry's after school for a Coke and "jitterbug" to a jukebox ... or maybe to the Texas or Diana Shoppe?

How many recall the ice house on Hale Street; remember Joe Wagner and following the ice truck on a hot summer day?

33

Charley Chambers riding his horse and buggy through town ... how about the scissors man pulling his cart through the streets?

By Sharon E. Bradley-Keller
Lewistown

A few years ago, before my mother passed away, we sat down and she recalled what she could about downtown Lewistown many years ago. She did a pretty good job of placing how many downtown stores there were in the 1950s and '60s and the names of each. She even recalled the order they were in on the street.

I can still see her sitting with her eyes closed going up Market Street in her mind, around the square and back down the other side of the street, tapping into her memory to place each one. As she recited them, I wrote them down and then she proofread it to me to make sure I got it correct. She missed a few, and someone reading this may be able to fill in the blanks, but she really recalled them well. I enjoyed sharing that with her and, to this day, am so happy I did.

So, on behalf of Marian L. Pecht, I am submitting her memory of downtown Lewistown and how our little town used to be long ago:

Downtown Lewistown in the '40s and '50s

Starting in the block before the post office, going toward and Square and Five Points:

Market Street
Kissinger Jewelry Store
Aresenui's Quick Lunch
Wolf Furniture
Post Office
A few other stores in here
Coleman Hotel
Headings Drug Store (one Headings brother)
Hofbrau Bar
Diane Candy and Restaurant
Texas (Laskaris)
MUR Jewelers (corner)

Market Street, Lewistown

Main Street
(Down Main Street - Embassy Theatre)
Murphy's (Lower 5&10)
Huffman's Bookstore (very tiny - big inventory)
State Restaurant
Rueben's Sporting Goods (hunting gear, cameras, etc.)
Dress shop
McCrory's 5&10
Famous Clothing Store
Past Time Theatre
Royal Jewelry Store and back hall, Jimmy Kepler Photography
Russell National Bank

Brown Street
Banker's Corner
Lewistown Trust Co.
Wian Shoes
Princess Shop
People's Drug Store
Hardware Store
Rea&Derrick Drug Store
G.C. Murphy (Upper 5&10)
Woolworth's

Danks & Co.

Five Points
Headings Drug Store (other brother)
Valley Street
Chandler's Hat Shop
Rodger's Jewelry Store
Another dress shop?
Another jewelry store
Back down Market Street (other side toward the Square)
Bowman's Furniture Store
Smith's Men's Store
First National Bank (BEFORE Banker's Corner - original location before the move)
Hugh B. McMeen Furniture Store
E.E. McMeen Department Store (Bon Ton now)
Goldman's Shop - women's clothing (one brother)
Joe Katz Men's Store
Bank (with clock, now gone)
Dandyline Shoe Store $$
Glick's Shoes - cheaper shoes (Dandyline and Glick's run by same people)
Goldman's Kid's Shop

Two little shops, possibly the Bumble Bee Boutique and Bill Kennedy's Men's Shop
  Wilson's Jewelry Store (original location)
  Penn Furniture Store
  Smart Woman's Clothing (later Mussettia's)
  Campbell's Diner (now Trolley Car)
  Bob Davis Men's Store
  Rialto Movie Theatre
  Marrone's Food Market
  Lawyer's offices

Main Street at the Square

Courthouse
Penelec Electric Co.
Montgomery Wards
White's Bicycle Shop
Billy Barker's Newstand
Jack & Jill Children's Clothing (upstairs - Haley's Photography)
  Joe the Motorist
  Corkins Restaurant
  Lewistown Sporting Goods
  Clark's Hardware
  Kitting's Furniture Store
  Jail
  Back to where we started, across the street from Wolf Furniture and the post office

By Dottie Ritter
Lewistown

My grandfather, Maurice Prettyleaf, and my father, Francis Prettyleaf, had the Lewistown Wholesale Grocery Co.
  They sold to small, family-owned stores.
  I lived at 203 Logan St. Across the street was my Uncle Charlie Hoffman's store, and at the other end of the street was Shimp's. My father went bankrupt when the supermarkets came in.

By Connie Moen
Lewistown

I remember when my mother, Dorothy Y. Searer, and I used to stand in long lines at the G.C. Murphy 5 & 10 store so my mother could purchase stockings during World War II.
  I well remember my dad, Hobert Searer, using gas rationing stamps to purchase gasoline for our automobile, too.

By Peggy Stewart Hetrick
McClure

I lived on Green Avenue, right beside Mrs. Gregg's Store. Bill and Mrs. Gregg had the greatest selection of

Teresa Orr, of Lewistown, submitted this photo in 2009 and explains: "I don't know the gentleman in the photo or even how I acquired this picture. If I had to guess, I would say it was probably among my grandmother's possessions and originally from her brother. I remember my great uncle Sam Miller lived in Lewistown and this may have been a friend of his. He is seen here along the Square in downtown Lewistown in front of the barbershop where the Juniata Valley Bank is currently located. You can see the side of the Courthouse on North Main Street in the background."

penny candy any little kid would love, and I did.
  I wish children today could experience having five pennies to pick out anything you wanted. The Greggs were so patient with the local children.
  I remember Lady Fingers, Mary Janes, Squirrels, Licorice, Bazooka gum and little metal trays of candy with a little spoon to eat it, teaberries, 1-cent a scoop, licorice pipes, red or black, plastic flying saucers that melted in your mouth, edible necklaces, too.
  I'll never forget the Southside and all my friends.

Tom Johnson Shoes

WILLIAM JOHNSON

"The Old Reliable Shoe Store"

"THEN"

William Johnson, the founder on right—Tom. S. Johnson, his Son, the present proprietor, Middle Figure

"NOW"

Queen Quality Shoes for Women
Walk-Over Shoes for Men and Women
Established 1851

112 E. Market Street

TOM S. JOHNSON   Proprietor

1925

Susan and Carl King, of Lewistown, have a vast collection of local memorabilia, which includes a shoelace hook, a 1984 pocket knife and two plastic merchandise bags from Tom Johnson's.

Another Tom Johnson bag, this one submitted by Jane Mort

More from T.J.'s

Jane Mort, of Mifflintown, was one of the winners of Tom Johnson Shoes wooden trucks in a 1993 promotion of the long-time downtown Lewistown business conducted by owner Jim Tunall. He signed and numbered the bottom.

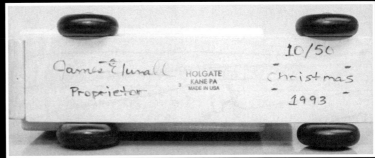

Tom Johnson Shoes

Excerpt from a 1994 advertisement in The Sentinel:

Tom Johnson Shoes in downtown Lewistown was honored during the 1989 bicentennial festivities as Mifflin County's oldest retail establishment.

In fact, T.J.'s is one of the 10 oldest operating shoe stores in the United States. The store was rated number eight in a national shoe retailers magazine, published in 1957.

The history of Tom Johnson and his father, William, has been documented in the press many times over the years. The longevity of the business owes a great deal to the ability of each owner to adjust and adapt to the needs and wants of his customers. From William's in-house shoe making, to son Tom's emphasis on service; Mel Bortell's expansion of brands and sizes, to current owner Jim Tunall's constant updating and improving the store.

As T.J.'s (Tom Johnson's registered nickname) moves forward

into the nineties, the decor and atmosphere does an about face and marches proudly into another era. Make it a "must see" to visit T.J.'s soon, where they have restored William's original counter and business desk. See today's finest fashionable lines displayed on Tom Johnson-era antiques, surrounded with shoe memorabilia of bygone days.

Relax among the oak collectibles, and wallow in service defined during Tom Johnson's tenure at the fitting stool.

More shoe stores

Some Points for Shoe Buyers.

Do you want Full Value for every cent you spend?
Do you want Service?
Do you want Style?
Do you want Satisfaction?
Do you want Bottom Prices?

If you do buy your Footwear of

J. CLARKE & SON,

15 East Market Street, - - Lewistown, Pa.

Stock Always Full, Prices Always Down.

Postcards from the collection of Chris Kearns, of Lewistown, include Christmas greetings from J. Clarke & Son shoe store, and the store itself, located on East Market Street in Lewistown. The postmark is dated Sept. 6, 1917.

An advertisement, left, for J. Clarke & Son was published in the 1894 book, "Lewistown, Penna., As It Is," by H. J. Fosnot, of the Sentinel and Democrat, reprinted here courtesy of Pam Goss, of Lewistown.

SHOE FITTERS For 3 Generations

Established 1859

CLARKE'S
15 EAST MARKET ST.

1925 ad

An advertisement for another long-time popular Lewistown shoe store, W.H. Wian, also appeared in the 1894 book.

The advertisement text states:

This is W.H. Wian, the popular boot and shoe man, of whom the "Brownie" is speaking, and trying to impress upon the minds of his companions the fact that WIAN carries in stock the largest and most complete line of footwear in Mifflin County. Two complete stores in one. On the first floor will be found the finest and very latest style shoes for men, women and children. The basement, which is one-half larger than the store proper, is devoted to heavy boots, lumberman's knit and felt goods, rubbers of every description and a full and complete line of trunks and valises of the most modern styles, at rock bottom prices.

This is **W. H. WIAN,** the popular Boot and Shoe Man, of whom the "Brownie" is speaking, and trying to impress upon the minds of his companions the Fact that WIAN carries in stock the largest and most complete line of Footwear in Mifflin County. Two complete stores in one. On the first floor will be found the finest and very latest style

SHOES FOR MEN, WOMEN AND CHILDREN.

The basement, which is one-half larger than the store proper, is devoted to

Heavy Boots, Lumberman's Knit and Felt Goods, Rubbers of every description and a full and complete line of TRUNKS AND VALISES of the most modern styles, at Rock Bottom Prices. Yours,

W. H. WIAN.

Photos submitted by Sharon Yetter

Shimp's, owned by Merril (Skinny) and Edith Shimp, was located at 228 Valley St., Lewistown.

By Sharon Yetter
Lewistown

In August 1958, Mr. and Mrs. Merril (Skinny) and Edith Shimp bought a small restaurant at 228 Valley Street, Lewistown. It was right beside the Acme store. They bought the shop from Vic and Dot Lidick.

Skinny, as everyone called him, operated the hoagie shop until retirement in August 1976.

Back in 1958, the soda cooler was an old Coca-Cola cooler that used blocks of ice to keep soda cold. The ice company came every other day with a block, and he chopped it in pieces, then he would drain the water out when it got too high.

His lunch menu was hoagies, or his barbecue, or his famous chili. He also had hot roast beef or pork sandwiches, with french fries and gravy. His hot dogs were different. He cooked them in the deep fryer, and they came out round so they would fit in his hamburger rolls.

The neighborhood kids would hang out and play the pinball machine and listen to the old juke box, which cost 5 cents for one play, or 10 for 25 cents. They would play for hours. They also ate lunch; half hoagie, 50 cents, pint of chocolate milk, 15 cents, and a Tastykake, 10 cents. A whole hoagie cost only $1.

Boys and girls would meet their boy and girl friends at the hoagie shop and sit in the last booth, and carve their names in hearts on the booth walls.

Many kids didn't have money for their lunch. He would always make them something and say, "You can pay later, or you can sweep the sidewalk, or wash the picture window."

When the kids graduated, they would always bring a name tag and a picture in for Skinny to put on the back wall in the middle of the shop. When he retired, he had collected over 200 pictures and cards.

"Skinny" Shimp sits at the counter at this shop.

"... Many kids didn't have money for their lunch. He would say, 'You can pay later, or you can sweep the sidewalk, or wash the picture window.' ..."

The outside sign shows that Shimp's sold Ka-Vee Ice Cream. Shimp's daughter, Sharon Yetter, still has the sign at the top of the page, and the iced tea cooler, pictured above.

Keepsakes from Lewistown

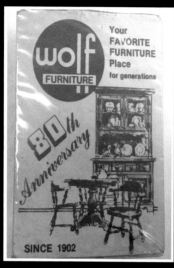

A still-wrapped deck of playing cards from Wolf Furniture Store, from the collection of Patsy Carson, Belleville.

Ashtray from McMeen's Department Store, Lewistown, from the collection of Patsy Carson, Belleville.

A Coble's Ice Cream lid from the collection of Randy Cutshall, Lewistown.

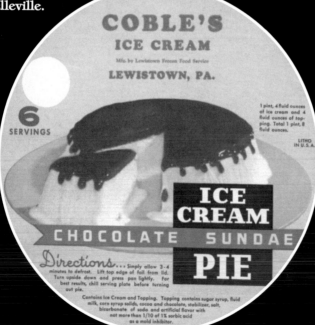

A Royale Dairy baby bottle from the collection of Randy Cutshall, Lewistown.

A Royale Dairy flyswatter from the collection of Susan and Carl King, Lewistown.

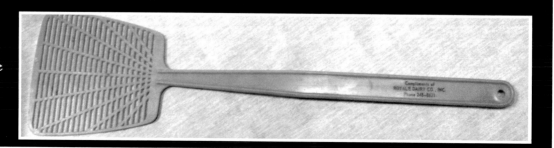

Entertaining business

RIALTO
SHRINE of the SILENT ART
RIALTO GRAND ORGAN

First
Anniversary
Week

FEBRUARY 11-16, 1924

SOUVENIR
PROGRAM

THE RIALTO THEATRE

By the courtesy of George M. Krupa of the Aldine and Hamilton Theatres, Lancaster, Pa.

GUEST ORGANIST

John S. Krupa
Organist Hamilton Theatre, Lancaster
Pupil of Ralph Kinder

Music at The Rialto

Good music has played a vital part in the history of the human race; but it is doubtful if its effect has ever been equaled by that created in a properly cued motion picture accompaniment, such as the Rialto affords. While the average spectator may be unaware of it, the best photoplays are always enhanced by suitable melodies; shifting, according to the organist's insight and intelligence, with the phases of the plot, from gay to grave, and from the ludicrous to the serene. Precisely this is accomplished with the **Rialto Grand Organ**.

Sondra Griffith, of Yeagertown, has in her collection of business memorabilia a 1924 souvenir program from the Rialto Theatre, and a 1920 Temple Theatre program. Both were in Lewistown.

1920

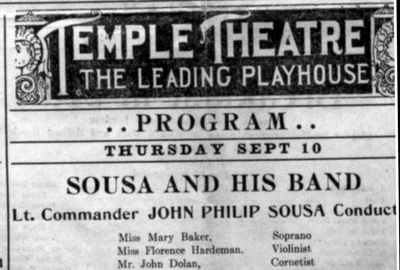

TEMPLE THEATRE
THE LEADING PLAYHOUSE

..PROGRAM..

THURSDAY SEPT 10

SOUSA AND HIS BAND

Lt. Commander JOHN PHILIP SOUSA Conduct

Miss Mary Baker,	Soprano
Miss Florence Hardeman,	Violinist
Mr. John Dolan,	Cornetist

Lewistown collectibles

Submitted by Susan and Carl King, Lewistown

Kirby's Restaurant

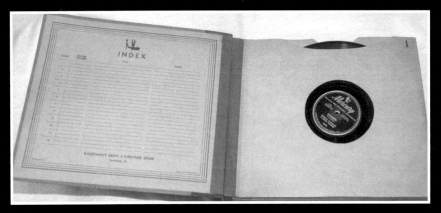

Kauffman's Music and Furniture Store

Gilliland Jewelers

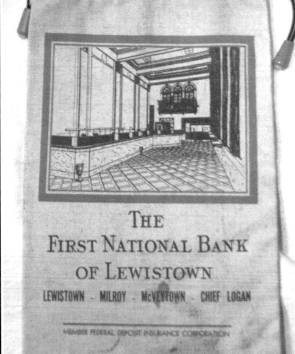

City Taxi

First National
Bank of Lewistown

Stetson hat

Riverside Wholesale

Russell National Bank

A trip down Memory Lane, Lewistown

By Dennis Sieber
Reedsville

Dutch's Diner was owned by "Dutch" Strawser, who lived on Maple Avenue. He was my boss at Standard Steel in the rigging gang.

The diner was well run by, I believe his wife, maybe a daughter, also, and I remember the frosted mugs with root beer. Homemade?

Marrone's had a very good grocery store near the Rialto Theater. Dick Berrier, who graduated with me in 1950, worked there as it was his life-long dream. He went later to Mifflintown and managed the grocery store there, later the supermarket there.

Joe Marrone was requested by Father Reilly every year to sing "Danny Boy" at the Sacred Heart St. Patrick's Day Show. The men there did a hilarious ballet dance with tutus. Also, Joe had a great voice and probably sang with my wife, Rosalie (Sieber).

I talked with him once on my mail route at his home on South Grand Street, and commented on the delicious aroma drifting out, and asked what his wife was making.

"Oh, that's the spaghetti sauce — I'm making a large pot of that every time we get low." His Italian mother's recipe.

We moved during World War II to East Fourth Street, above Thoman's Auto Store. We had the miniature village "Fairyland" in our back yard. Built on the limestone cliff by the former owner, Mr. Bottomly, and his neighbor, Homer Searer. They even had electric lights in them at that time.

On Valley Street at that time was Lew Himes' gas station at the corner of Valley and Pine. There also was Speedy Cleaners, Bowman's Furniture, a barber shop and Bergey's Store. A block away was Mary Carter Paint Store, Henry's Hardware, Mr. Knepp's Clothing, Dimeo's Barbershop, Zampelli's TV Store and Stade's Music Shop.

Down below, on Logan, Shaw and Pannebaker Avenue, were Shimp's Store and multiple mom and pop stores, barber shops and beauty shops, as were on most of the streets in town. I could go on and on, but names sometimes evade my memory.

A few more: Hillside Drug Store (Fleisher's), Lawler's Bar, Royal Jewelers (I worked there two days at $5/week), Lembo's Winery, Roy Long's Hobby Shop, Mur's Jewelry, McClure's Jewelry, Wilson's Jewelry, Leora's on South Dorcas Street, at one time, maybe the 1920s, a Chinese laundry across on Dorcas Street, Gilliland's Jewelry near Hower's Cleaners, Superior Ice and Co. (South Main Street? Their phone number 835 is on an ice pick I have), Coble's Ice Storage (butcher, too?), coal yards on Montgomery Avenue, and many others.

Don't forget: Arrow Shirt Factory (my father-in-law, Andy Guy, ran it at one time), Cox's Bowling Alley, Basom's Store on South Main Street, Hoage Groceries, later Silkman's, Dick Wagner's Cafe, Klinger's Restaurant (at Snedeker Oil now), Martin's Grill, Fritz Funeral Home at Five Points, both Headings Drug Stores, Pyle's Store at Spruce and Walnut, Daisy Corner and Sassaman's Gas and Oil.

Downtown Lewistown

Allene Fleck, of Lewistown, shares memorabilia from downtown Lewistown shoe stores: a box from J.S. Raub circa mid 1960s-70s; and a clacker and clown game from Kinney Shoes from 1940.

Dutch's Diner began as a frozen custard stand

By Bev Strawser Manbeck
York
Daughter of Ray "Dutch" and
Margaret Strawser

My parents had Dutch's Diner. It all started with a free-standing frozen custard stand next to where they put the diner (South Brown Street, Lewistown). It was a trailer, a custard machine that was built into a trailer. My dad and a friend, Harold Amspacker, drove out west to get it, and they brought it back. From that, he decided he was going to build a restaurant.

They had the custard machine around 1947 or '48, and built the diner itself very soon afterwards, about 1950 or '51.

I remember the knotty pine booths.

Dad worked at the Standard (Standard Steel in Burnham). Mom (Margaret Strawser) didn't drive, so he took her in early in the morning. In the early days, they kept the diner opened until midnight.

He didn't work in the diner, but did the paperwork. My mother joked that she did the work and he took the money home.

The best-selling meal was a hamburger, french fries and homemade baked lima beans for 50 cents. And there always was homemade pie. The homemade pies were really popular.

We had a big root beer barrel; it must have been about three feet high. They put the mugs in a type of freezer. When we took one out and drew a root beer, the whole mug would frost up, and, if you were lucky, you would get little slivers of ice from the frost in your mug. It was very cold. The root beer was kept cold inside the barrel, too.

When he had the custard machine, he had a special mix from the Royale

Photo courtesy Mifflin County Historical Society
Dutch's Diner

Dairy. Unfortunately, it died with my dad; he never shared it. It wasn't as hard as ice cream, and it wasn't as soft as soft ice cream; it was truly a frozen custard. They still served it when they opened the diner.

The only reason the diner closed was when redevelopment came through around 1968 and you had to buy into it. My mother decided that she was too old and didn't do it, but she later regretted it. She continued to do some catering and making the homemade pies, but she just didn't

enjoy it like she did the diner.

I remember on Sundays, like Easter, when all the family was around, we all had dinner at the diner. It was fun.

I am so proud of my parents, they both only went as far as sixth grade.

Now, my daughter has the old Pepsi chalkboard that my mom used to write the specials on, and I just visited her and we used an ice cream dipper from the diner. Every one of us has dishes or something from the diner.

Mur Jewelry Store was once located in the Taft Hotel on Monument Square, Lewistown.

Mur Jewelry Store relocated many times

By Steve Zewe
Lewistown

My dad, Regis J. Zewe, managed the Mur Jewelry Store after arriving here from McKeesport, Pennsylvania, after he attended watch repair school after World War II (I worked there cleaning windows, floors etc., when I was around 8 or 10 years of age).

The store received water damage when a man fell asleep in the Taft Hotel (his room was above the store) while smoking.

Dad then relocated to Chestnut Street for a short period of time, then to McCory's when they went out of business (was robbed when he was there, someone came through the suspended ceiling), and then relocated across the street to one of the stores that were recently torn down to make way for the new CVS.

I think the store that he relocated to was the Video Vendor, who moved in after Mur's closed. Dad was robbed there, too, by an armed man.

Time flies.

An advertisement for the National Hotel, later called the Taft Hotel, was published in the 1894 book, "Lewistown, Penna., As It Is," by H. J. Fosnot, of the Sentinel and Democrat, reprinted here courtesy of Pam Goss, of Lewistown.

B. F. Goodrich Silvertown Stores

15 South Dorcas Street

Lewistown

By Jack Shuey
Lewistown

The hatless man wearing the vest was E.E. Keemer, manager. The man in uniform was my dad, Robert Shuey Sr., probably 1943. Dad went into the U.S. Navy shortly after this and worked there also after the war.

Interior of the store

Shilling's Sheet Metal: A family business

By Todd A. Shilling
Reedsville

My great-grandfather was William J. Shilling, born in 1890, who started the business in 1919. Prior to that he was a motorman for the Trolley Company.

The information we have is that he was on Valley Street, Lewistown, near Five Points, then moved to 15 North Main Street (across the alley from the McCoy House, where the Juniata Valley Bank is now located). He was there until sometime in early 1930.

We just found out last year that in 1930 he built the shop on top of Valley Street, at 664 Valley Street. I have the blueprints for this building. His son, (my grandfather), Robert W. Shilling Sr., worked for his dad until W.J. Shilling turned the business over to him around 1960.

When Robert W. Shilling Sr. took over the business in 1960, the name was changed to Shilling's Sheet Metal Contractor.

My dad, Rodger Shilling, and his

William J. Shilling

Robert W. Shilling

younger brother, Robert Shilling Jr., worked for their dad, until late 1970. My dad was making $2.15 an hour at the time, and had been making $1.25 an hour in 1960 at the age of 18.

In January 1973, my grandfather, Robert W. Shilling, passed away suddenly. The building and contents of the shop were sold. The building at 664 Valley Street still stands today. It has two apartments in it now.

Photos submitted by Todd A. Shilling. More on next page.

As a small child of 5 or 6, I remember going in to the Shop, as my father called it, and I to this day still call it that. I remember getting on these Fairbanks scales every time I would go in to the shop. It's just something that always stuck in my mind, so I am very happy and proud to have this back in the family. These date back to the 1920s. They used this scale to weigh anything made from sheet metal, or iron, as my great-grandfather, W. J. Shilling, called it, to figure out a price. So I proudly have these scales in my living room to look at and enjoy every day.

— *Todd A. Shilling*

Early 1930s

RETURN AFTER FIVE DAYS TO
W. J. SHILLING

TINNING, ROOFING, SPOUTING
664 VALLEY STREET
LEWISTOWN, PENNA.

Shilling's Sheet Metal had a Chevrolet truck, possibly a 1962 model, in the mid-1960s, above.

The business in the photo below is pictured in the early to mid-1960s.

The Hattie Meyers column published in The Sentinel in 1973 contains some of the family's history.

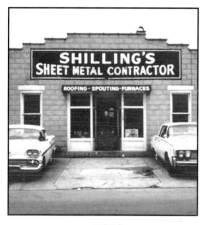

1960s

Photos and newspaper clipping submitted by Todd A. Shilling

we Notice that:

The Mocker sings!
The Shillings step in

By HATTIE MEYERS

Listen to the Mockingbird! Listen to the Mockingbird! The Mockingbird is singing all the day.

And did you know that even in the darkest of nights, the Mockingbird's little heart thrills with joy and he breaks forth in song?

Another thing you may not have known is that he is fond of human society, thrives well in captivity and is a common and popular pet.

Perhaps you have never been made acquainted with this beautiful and friendly creature of the feathered world who is known to mimic with success the songs of other birds.

So it may be in order to introduce you. It represents a genus of thrushlike wrens and its plumage is all bluish-gray and white. It has been called a Mimic Thrush and has gained its worldwide reputation as a songster strictly on its merits.

To help you recognize him, he is about 9 to 11 inches in length. The upper parts are dark and bluish gray and the longish tipped tail is edged with white. The wings have two white wingbars and white wing patch.

The underparts are light gray. This feathered friend of ours has varied songs arising from imitating the songs of other birds and even imitating the noises of the neighborhood. One of his odd-ball characteristics is to repeat each phrase at least a dozen times before going on to the next.

Here is a bird which seems to live to sing. Yes, the Mocker is never reluctant to pour out its torrent of notes; sweet, clear, sharp, grating, harsh, high, low or hushed; day or night, spring, summer, fall or even in the dead of winter. Indeed this sprightly one seems to live to sing.

wnt

Mocker needed Help

Margaret Shilling Fisher, former Mifflin County school teacher and wife of Robert P. Fisher of Pleasant Acres, sparked off this story when she phoned me about a baby mockingbird some boys had found near her home and brought to her for help. She says that through the years and more recently they have had pairs of mockingbirds in the bush and trees near their home.

We well remember Margaret's father, William J. Shilling, for nearly 50 years, conducting one of the leading Sheet Metal businesses in the county, first on Valley near Five Points, later on North Main Street and finally on Stratfords Hill, Valley Street where his son Robert conducted the business after his father's retirement till Robert's death January of this year.

William Shilling is well remembered as a great hunter and baseball fan. He served on the Yeagertown School Board for 12 years and as board president for four years.

Even after retirement he couldn't become a quitter but every morning made his way to his place of business to watch the workers and per chance sometimes do a little overseeing.

His wife, the former Pearl Kauffman died 1916.

His son Robert's first wife, the former Beulah Goss died 1968. His widow is the former Alice Shellenberger of Milroy.

Robert has three sons, Richard married to Margery Esh; Rodger is wed to Sally Harmon and they have three children children, and Robert Shilling and the former Connie Wray have two children.

Robert P. Fisher is the son of John and Nellie Pry Fisher of West Fifth Street. He will be remembered as a driver for railway express when Luther Wyland was the express agent and also with the Howard Kline Auto Parts business on Valley Street.

He served with the medical corps in the U.S. Army with Patton's Tank Corps which was used in the liberation of Buchenwald.

wnt

The Birds and I Are Confused

It seems there's so much confusion all around us that even the birds are affected. The other night I suddenly got awake at 9:15, thought I had slept all night and was preparing to dress and start pounding these keys when a few queries and doubts arose. I made a phone call and found I had slept only two hours.

Others agree with me that last Winter the birds did not patronize the feeders as usual. We wondered if they had a way of getting live food. Anyway we wished for their company and chirps.

Now the summer birds are here galore morning night and noon, expecting me to give them all social security for all their babies and clannish groups while they enjoy life as mere playboys and playgirls. Can you beat that one? Nothing but confusion all around!

On the south side of town

South Side Hoagie Shop

Information and photos submitted by Jeannie (Rocco) Wagner and Samuel E. Rocco
Lewistown

South Side Hoagie Shop is a family-owned landmark in Lewistown, Pennsylvania, that has been serving the freshest hoagies for more than 70 years. Started by Joseph and Cuba Anastasia in 1947, the original recipes are still used today.

Joe and Cuba started with a small mom and pop grocery deli at 329 S. Main St., in Lewistown. After the building suffered substantial damage as a result of a fire, they moved their business next door to 327 S. Main St., only to encounter another fire in the apartment above the store, forcing them to close and begin remodeling, where it became the hoagie shop as it is known today.

Knowing Rocco's Super Market was opening in the near future, they knew they could not compete with them on groceries, so they changed their focus to hoagies and sandwiches. After a trip to Philadelphia, Joe came back with the idea to name

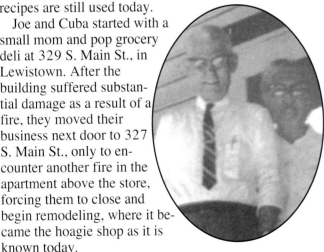

Joseph and Cuba Anastasia

Rocco's Market

By Jeannie (Rocco) Wagner
Family history provided by Samuel E. Rocco
Photos submitted by Joseph Rocco, Susan (Rocco) Green and Jeannie (Rocco) Wagner

Frank and Mary Raccuia moved from Sicily, Italy, to Renovo, Pennsylvania, in the early 1900s, where they opened a small grocery store. While living in Renovo, they ran their store, grew and sold their own produce, and raised chickens, all while Frank and some of his sons worked in the brickyards of Renovo until they closed.

As new immigrants to America, they adapted to their new home by changing their name from Raccuia to Rocco because people had difficulty pronouncing and spelling their name.

After the brickyards closed, the Roccos moved their family to Lewistown, Pennsylvania, in 1927, where they started a couple of small "mom and pop" shops on Wayne and Dorcas streets, on the south side of Lewistown.

In 1932, they built their homestead and a small grocery store and meat market named Rocco's

Frank and Mary Rocco

the new shop "Anastasia's Submarines." Only after he was told he could not use that name ("submarine" was trademarked), he changed the name to "South Side Hoagie Shop."

The Anastasias ran the business for 13 years before selling it to their cousin, Charles Rocco, in 1960, who, with his wife, Verna, continued the South Side tradition for another 12 years. After Verna's passing and the flood of 1972, the shop was closed down for a year and a half until Charles sold the business to Samuel E. Rocco and Jean Rocco, his nephew and his wife.

After renovating the building and reopening the business on Dec. 6, 1973, Sam and Jean worked the shop together with family, selling hoagies, cheesesteaks, cold and hot sandwiches, burgers, chicken and salads, until Jean's death in September 1997.

It was in September 2000 when Samuel finished his 27th year in business and sold it to his daughter, Jeannie (Rocco) Wagner, and her husband, Bryson Wagner Jr., who still own and operate the business today, continuing the tradition of serving the freshest hoagies, now for more than 70 years.

Samuel E. and Jean Rocco

Charles Rocco

Bryson and Jeannie (Rocco) Wagner

Advertisement in The Sentinel, Lewistown, Aug. 22, 1949

Store at 345 S. Main St., Lewistown. This was home to Rocco's Store until March of 1949, when they built Rocco's Super Market in the lot beside it.

Rocco's Super Market was a state-of-the-art facility that was renowned for its fresh cut meats, produce and customer service. One of its amenities included "baggers," who bagged your groceries and took them to your car for you.

Home delivery was another service they offered their customers, and they made many deliveries in the Lewistown, Burnham, Yeagertown, Reedsville and surrounding areas over the years. They even made deliveries by boat across the Juniata River to residents of Hawstone before there was a road to Lewistown.

Upon Frank's death in 1959, Rocco's Super Market was carried on by his children until 1977, when it was purchased by Samuel E. Rocco and Jean Rocco, Frank and Mary's grandson and wife. Rocco's Super Market was a family-owned and operated business that thrived for almost 30 years before a tragic fire destroyed the business in May of 1978.

Noerr Motor Freight

Company's long history dates back to 1927

*Submitted by Scott A.N. Noerr
Lewistown*

From the Noerr Motor Freight 50th anniversary booklet, printed in 1977:

Out of the coal mining region of Pennsylvania, from a small town, Punxsutawney, comes the history of Noerr Motor Freight Inc. Let us go back to the beginning, the very start of a family known as Noerr: Frank B. and Mabel Noerr, father and mother of Floyd B., Mary, George M. and Clair B., living in the small coal mining town.

Frank B., hereafter referred to as Pap, knew coal mining all his life, working the mines as well as owning a coal mine in Jefferson County, providing for his family through hard work in the black rock mountain, holding an aptitude for a business venture as yet unknown to him or his family.

Back in those days, coal was sent by rail to many towns. Lewistown was one of those towns receiving coal for heating purposes, and coincidentally, was the home of Clair's wife, Mary.

In 1926, Pap and Clair, with his wife, Mary, moved to Lewistown. Pap stayed with Mary's family, the Barnetts, for a time, eventually moving in with Clair and Mary when they were settled into an apartment. Mabel did not come to Lewistown, but chose to stay in her hometown of Punxsutawney, while Pap ventured out into the world of business with his vast knowledge of coal.

Weekend visits were made by Pap to his wife and home, and he continued this arrangement until her death.

Noerr Motor Freight 50th anniversary booklet

Later, Pap had her body reinterred in Lewistown, where he had now made his home.

Enthusiastic in their attempts at business, Pap and Clair followed the advice of the Barnetts and contacted Ken Hile, whose family operated a coal yard on Walnut Street. Telling Ken of their hopes to start a coal and dray business, but not knowing of an adequate location, they were quickly told about an old vacant flour mill located on Mill Street owned by a Mr. Wisup. After meeting with Mr. Wisup, they agreed to lease the mill. One major reason for leasing the mill was due to the fact that scales were provided for use in the coal production.

In 1927, a father and son together built a business and called it F.B. Noerr and Son. Starting with one

Model T pick-up truck, the father and son team began the process of shipping coal from Punxsutawney to Lewistown by rail, unloading the coal at the tipple on Mill Street.

Christening the new establishment F.B. Noerr and Son, they were off to a flying start.

Before long, a second Model T Ford dump truck was purchased and, foreseeing an opportunity for hauling furniture, a Dodge Stake-body truck was bought.

In 1929, despite hard times, a new customer is found. The American Viscose Corp., a producer of rayon yarn, shipped their product by rail, but due to a rush order, was put in a bit of a bind. They needed a load of yarn delivered to Concordia Knitting Mills near Beverly, N.J. As they could not wait for the rails to deliver the load, they took a chance, and called F.B. Noerr and Son, coal merchants and draymen.

Agreeing to deliver the yarn, they quickly took charge, loading the yarn at the American Viscose Corp., they covered the truck with a tarpaulin to protect the yarn from the weather. The delivery was made promptly and without complications, and due to the success of the trip, F.B. Noerr and Son was soon asked to deliver more and more loads for the rayon manufacturers, thereby establishing a steady business relationship between the two.

Lewistown's Mayor John Lawler, 83 years young, is credited for making out the first business transaction. As a young clerk, he recalls Bill Black and brother, Hen, as two of the first drivers for F. B. Noerr and Son.

The 1930s established the trucking industry as it is known today, not because times were good, rather because they were bad. The turbulence, chaos and destructive competition which marred the industry eventually made it necessary to unify the industry. There were several futile efforts toward unity, but ultimately, on Oct. 1, 1933, The American Trucking Association was formed.

The responsible members of the in-

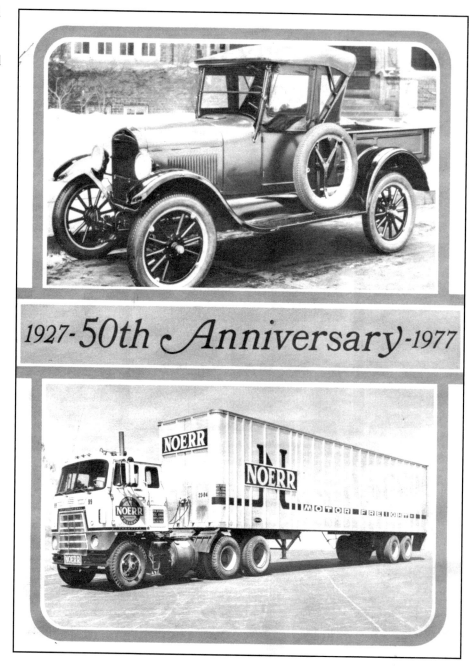

1927-*50th Anniversary*-1977

Noerr Motor Freight 50th anniversary booklet

dustry then asked for federal regulation, which was accomplished in the Motor Carrier Act of 1935. This regulated tariffs, routes, schedules, finances, licenses and other pertinent aspects of carriers operating in interstate commerce. States followed with similar legislation, and the trucking industry moved from turbulence to stability.

Pennsylvania established, by act of legislature, the Public Utility Commission, which required all persons,

corporations or partnerships that had been doing business and wanted to continue to do business, as a common carrier or a carrier for a company or group of companies, to apply for a certificate of authority to the newly created Public Utility Commission.

At this time, an application was filed by F.B. Noerr and Son for Grandfather Rights to cover the type of hauling that they had been doing. This certificate was granted.

Many applications were filed, for

F.B. "Pap" Noerr

Clair B. "Dude" Noerr

Floyd B. Noerr

the Noerr Company, with the PUC and ICC for additional rights. Most of these applications were contested by other certificated carriers, and this resulted in many hearings they were held in which a representative of the Noerr Company and their attorney, Paul S. Lehman, attended throughout Pennsylvania and the middle atlantic states.

As a result of those hearings, the Noerr Company established either general or specific rights to serve the general public and rights to serve specific customers for the eastern part of the United States.

During these years, sub-marginal firms went out of business or were sold to more successful carriers. Many of the leased operations that were hauling for F.B. Noerr and Son were eventually disbanded, although one of the earliest, Shuman L. Wright, survived the struggle.

Beginning his career on Decoration Day, 1933, he drove to Pittsburgh, Pa., with his first load. In 1934, with his one truck, a GMC straight job, he first leased his services to F. B. Noerr and Son. By 1935, he had purchased his second truck. In 1936, he bought his first trailer. First hauling freight, later hauling rayon yarn for American Viscose, he is, 43 years later, still leasing to the Noerr Company, today hauling polyester, fiberglass and steel.

As time went on, F.B. Noerr and Son took on a more business-like ap-

pearance. Their growth accelerated. Outgrowing their home on Mill Street, they temporarily moved to the old cannery building on Shaw Avenue, but soon moved to Bill Baker's Garage on Walnut Street in 1934. Still progressing, they relocated in the old trolley barns on Electric Avenue for motor purposes and repair service.

Another son makes the scene. On October 19, 1936, George M., together with brother Clair, purchased a tract of land on South Main Street at Jack's Creek and U.S. 22. A new structure was built housing Noerr's Garage; they acquired the GMC Franchise for General Motors Trucks. A terminal was included to provide service for F. B. Noerr and Son. The two

separate companies operated under the same roof until after they were incorporated, and Noerr Motor Freight Inc., moved to their new location at 205 Washington Avenue, Lewistown, in 1964.

During this time, another son, Floyd B.. had become involved with the company. Playing an active part in the business, he commuted to Lewistown from Punxsutawney, where he had worked for the American Railway Express.

Political minded and management wise, he contributed greatly to the accelerated growth of the business. Planting his feet firmly into the business, he eventually bought out Pap's interest in the company. Upon Pap's

First truck to bear the F.B Noerr and Son name.

retirement in 1941, a new partnership was formed. Floyd B. now joined Clair to run the company.

Clair, a very successful public relations man, made many trips seeking new territory and customers; Floyd took over the management. Working together with their own individual skills, they soon were turning F.B. Noerr and Son into a prosperous enterprise.

Come 1950, a change takes place. F.B. Noerr and Son became incorporated, giving way to a new organizational name, Noerr Motor Freight Inc. Clair B. became the president; Floyd's son, Robert, became vice president; Donald, another son of Floyd's, became secretary; and Floyd served as treasurer.

Political minded Floyd served on many local political committees, as well as activating himself in national trucking organizations. He served as president of the Motor Truck Association at the time when the trucking industry filed suit against the Eastern Railroad Association, January 17, 1953.

The now famous legal case, Noerr Motor Freight Inc., et al versus Eastern Railroad President's Conference, et al was heard in the United States District Court for the Eastern District of Pennsylvania. Noerr Motor Freight Inc. was named the number one company in the $2.5 million suit.

Noerr was followed by the other trucking companies chipping in their share to help legalize the tandem tractor-trailer. After the refusal of Governor Fines to sign the bill legalizing the tandem, an angry Floyd promoted an investigation of Byoir Associates, an advertising agency for the Eastern Railroad.

Disclosing false fronts and signatures on memos providing proof of the written consent for these falsifications revealed an admitted suppressing of the trucking companies to use tandem tractor-trailers. The $0.18 settlement was a depressant financially, but the initial winning was a stimulant to the trucking industry. The tandem tractor-trailer gave the truckers the advantage

Richard C. Noerr

of competing with the railroads by enabling them to haul more weight and thus gain more revenue.

Floyd was elected president in 1957 following the death of Clair (Dude). He presided until his death in 1965. The bold leadership of this man will long be remembered as a stepping stone in the growth and development of a company called Noerr.

Donald G., young son of Floyd's begins working for F.B. Noerr and Son, and Noerr's Garage on his birthday, June 19, 1938. Starting his work experience pumping gas and helping to deliver freight, he has come a long way in the trucking firm; add lots of hard work as truck driver, dock worker, dispatcher, office worker and whatever else was associated with trucking, and you have the vice president of today's Noerr Motor Freight Inc.

Yesterday's experience has brought Donald Noerr through soon-to-be 40 years service with the company, an asset for the continued growth of Noerr Motor Freight Inc.

From the beginning, Clair B. Noerr was in on the action. President of Noerr Motor Freight Inc. from 1950 until his death in 1957; nicknamed Dude because of his western flair style of dress, which included a Stetson hat and puttees (leather leggings), which he wore, particularly when he was driving a truck. ...

Throughout his years, he established a well-deserved respect for his work, and courageous fortitude. He played an active part in national trucking organizations, as well as participating to the fullest with the PUC. By nature, Dude was a practical joker, and an ardent sportsman, a combination adding pleasure to the many that knew him.

A key figure in starting the freight transportation business, his attributes will forever play an important part of the heritage of Noerr Motor Freight Inc.

Richard C. Noerr, president of Noerr Motor Freight Inc., 1977. Always interested in trucking. As a very young lad, Richard Noerr was fascinated by trucks, always hanging around the terminals, dreaming of the day when he could get his hands into the business of trucking. That day arrived in 1948, when he officially began working for F.B. Noerr and Son.

Far from the sophisticated management dream, he started on the dock. Along with a fellow worker, Tom Leach, they first started a night-term shift, whereby trucks were unloaded at night.

He got experience learning traffic department work, rating bills. Leaving to pursue a college education, he was back within a year and a half to do what was foremost in his mind, trucking. Back to the docks, and then becoming a driver on pick up and delivery.

When a strike developed, he went on over-the-road driving. He was then married and about 1951 became safety engineer. Becoming vice president around 1953, he established a complete safety program, established maintenance records and a maintenance program.

After the departure of Robert Noerr, he gained the responsibilities of his job, taking over regulatory details, purchasing equipment, Philadelphia sales, and operations.

After Floyd's death in 1965,

Richard C. Noerr was elected president, and a lifetime dream came true. Enthusiasm had a lot to do with it, for Richard Noerr always had the desire to run the firm, and he has had that particular pleasure for the last 12 years.

...

Addendum

By Scott A. Noerr
Lewistown

From 1977 to 1986, the truckload divisions, including flatbeds, vans, refrigerated trailers and specialty trailers increased to over 500, with 150 company-owned tractors, and 150 owner operators.

In the early 1980s, the local deliver operation was shut down, but the nationwide truckload operation still flourished.

From 1983 to 1984, deregulation became an extremely negative effect on committed transportation lanes, and insurance costs nearly tripled, causing net profitability to degrease.

For two years, Noerr Motor Freight Inc. struggled, unbeknownst to most employees, and in 1986, owner Richard C. Noerr Sr., announced the company was filing Chapter 13. Noerr Motor Freight Inc. operated for almost a year, until all assets were liquidated in 1987.

Lewistown Borough purchased the maintenance building and some land to house their Refuse Department and equipment. The Borough Refuse Department still operates from this location in 2017.

Also, the main terminal was purchased and converted into a church and day care center. The church and day care center are still located there in 2017.

Scott A.N. Noerr, grandson of Richard C. Noerr, keeps memorabilia from Noerr Motor Freight in his office at Norlin Warehousing Services Inc., Lewistown, a business that was started by his grandfather, Don Noerr and Don Linn, in 1967.

An aerial view of Noerr Motor Freight submitted by Scott A. Noerr shows the location of the company along the Juniata River in Lewistown.

Smith's Atlantic Service Station

By Carl Smith
Lewistown

Corner of Market and Grand

The corner of Market and Grand in Lewistown, currently the home of Supportive Concepts, has seen many different buildings and businesses over the years. Not many locals likely remember that from 1936 or 1937 until June 20, 1951, that site was the home of Smith's Atlantic Service Station, which was run by my dad, Cloyd C. Smith.

When Dad began his lease of the station, the only structure there was a small office that sat at an angle in the back corner of the lot. As noted on the one large billboard sized sign, a major part of most service station business back then were chassis lubrications and oil changes. Since there was no garage for working indoors, those services were done with cars parked over a pit. Cars would be carefully driven over the pit and the mechanics would go down steps or a step ladder into the pit to do the oil change or lube.

Also, other work that was done outside and in all types of foul weather, was new and used tire installation and flat tire repairs. All of the tire work was done with tire bars and hammers; the high tech tire machines used in tire shops today were many years away.

Another interesting item that I remember Dad talking about was car radio installation because car radios were not a common "factory" item in many cars back then. The radio, AM only, was mounted in the dash and the speaker, which was quite large and bulky, got mounted under the dash. I still have a new, in the box, Motorola AM radio and speaker from those days.

I have no idea what year the major renovations were made to the service

Photo submitted by Carl Smith

Smith's Atlantic Service Station at the corner of Market and Grand streets, Lewistown

station while Dad was there, but the later photographs were taken after the original building was torn down and replaced by a much larger and nicer office and a modern two-bay service garage added where the guys could do their work out of the weather.

The signage at the station has many interesting features. The earlier photos show an elaborate, lighted Atlantic sign, which was later replaced by a much plainer steel pole and a flat metal Atlantic sign. The earlier photos also show that Atlantic sponsored baseball broadcasts on radio. Another sign that I found particularly

When Cloyd Smith began leasing the station, the only structure there was a small office that sat at an angle in the back corner of the lot. It was later replaced with a larger office and a two-bay service garage, below.

interesting was the one that indicates that Atlantic Credit Cards were honored there. I wasn't aware that credit cards were in use that long ago. Also, the large pyramid-like displays of oil and anti freeze are interesting and only possible because the station was open 24/7.

A close examination of the photos shows some of the "name" products that were sold back then. The tire of choice was the Lee brand, which was

a very popular tire brand for many years. Their slogan was "Lee of Conshohocken," as the tires were built in the town of Conshohocken, Pennsylvania. Some of the tires in those photos are completely wrapped in a course, light brown paper, which was common in the tire industry for many years. Other signs that are readable include Exide batteries and Motorola radios.

One of my favorite pictures is the

Cloyd Smith, left, and Earl Orner stand in the doorway of the office.

one of my dad and Earl Orner "posing" together at the front door of the office. The sign above them lists the proprietor as C. Cloyd Smith, which was a little name change that Dad liked to use at his businesses. In other words, when the need for gas or auto service arose, "See (C.) Cloyd Smith." Yes, a little corny, I suppose, but Dad liked it.

Dad closed the Market Street station, as well as his other one on West Fourth Street, on June 20, 1951. The grind of the two businesses, the extremely long hours and the constant "gas wars" were taking their toll. The Market Street station was later leveled and updated to a more modern Atlantic station. I believe the station had a couple different proprietors until it was finally shut down. The only one that I can remember was a friend of Dad's, a Mr. Shearer, who was there for several years. The building that is there now and is home to Supportive Concepts was, I believe, the original location of D.P. Music Store.

West Fourth Street

The building on West Fourth Street in Lewistown, which currently houses Bossert's Hardware and the Dan Pierce Outdoor Shop, plus four apartments, has a fascinating history.

Sadly, nearly everyone who was involved in its beginnings is now gone.

The original building was designed and built by my dad, Cloyd C. Smith, in the mid 1940s. When it first opened, in late December of 1946, it was the home of Smith's Hardware and Atlantic Service Station. Soon after, an additional section was added to the west end of the building, which was home to an Aunt Nellie's Grocery Store. The gas station was Dad's second location in town as he was also renting an Atlantic station on the corner of Market and Grand streets, across the street from the current Harvey Smith's Barber Shop.

The gas station on West Fourth Street was a three-bay facility and was

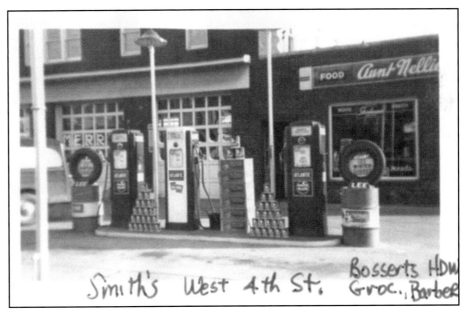

Photo submitted by Carl Smith

Smith's West Fourth Street, Lewistown, location

originally managed by Eugene Orner. Gene's brother, Earl, who would later become a major part of the Fourth Street building, was managing the Market Street gas station and Dad took on the hardware business. Dad soon found out that he did not like the hardware business and, as luck would have it, one of his good friends, Sam Bossert, was working at a local hardware and was anxious to go out on his own, which led to the introduction of Bossert's Hardware.

In 1951, Dad had tired of the gas business and decided to close the Fourth Street station and end his rent of the Market Street station.

Meanwhile, Bossert's hardware was doing well, and the Aunt Nellie's Grocery Store was, too. The grocery store was run by another of Dad's friends, Robert Kise Sr. At about the same time as Dad was getting out of the gas business, Kise had the opportunity to go full time with the A&P grocery store chain and, since Dad was closing both stations, that would mean that Earl Orner would be out of a job. So, with absolutely no experience in the grocery business, Earl decided to give it a try. As it turned out, that was a great move for both Earl and the residents of the "West End" as they, along with so many other locals,

got to enjoy 35 years of dealing with one of the all-time greatest jokesters and a great friend, from 1951 until his retirement on his birthday on July 4, 1986.

Bossert's Hardware and Orner's Lake Park Grocery, which had become a Clover Farm store, became mainstays, while other parts of the building saw many different businesses over the years.

After closing the gas station, Dad ran his Smith Tire and Battery Wholesale out of that section of the building for a few years.

A couple other businesses that I can recall there prior to the Outdoor Shop were Dean's Janitor Supply and Ripkas' Restaurant. The janitor supply was a local janitorial service owned by Mr. Dean (can't recall his first name) and Danny Wagner. They had started out in the back of one of the garages in Dad's building across the street behind what was then Hess Atlantic Station. As their business expanded, they needed more room so they moved into the building between the hardware and grocery store.

After the janitor supply moved on, that building was home to Ripka's Restaurant, which was run by Gene and Bessie(?) Ripka who were from Strodes Mills. Probably their biggest claim to fame was the fantastic hoagie business they developed. After the Ripkas closed their restaurant, Earl and Hazel Orner, with the help of the Ripkas sharing their hoagie "recipe," also became very well known for their hoagies at the grocery store on Friday and Saturday each week.

There was a small section of the building that had its own entrance next to the doorway that led upstairs to the four apartments. That room also held several businesses over the years, including one that would go on to become a Lewistown landmark business.

But, the first business in that room was a barber shop, which was run in the early '50s by George Mowery, another of Dad's good friends. George ran the shop for only a few years. After the barber shop closed, Dad opened a television store in that same room. In the early '50s not that many folks had televisions yet. I remember that on Friday and Saturday evenings, Dad would always have one or two sets turned on in the front window. Many of the locals would walk to the store, some would even drive there, and they would watch the Gillette Friday night boxing and Saturday night professional wrestling. It was almost like a mini drive-in and was a great sales gimmick, as it helped Dad sell many Motorola televisions.

After the television store closed, that room saw a couple other important businesses. One of those was the local Girl Scout office and the other was to become a true Lewistown landmark. I have no idea now what year it occurred, but a businessman from, I think, Tyrone, approached Dad with the idea of opening one of the very first area pizza shops, which was called Hi Way Pizza. The pizza shop was a great success, but after a few years the owner decided to sell the Lewistown shop. After some negotiations, Hi Way Pizza sold to Gus Hess, and thus began the locally famous and still popular Gus's Pizza.

The upstairs of the building had, and still has, four apartments. Back in the 1960s, when my brother and I were in high school, we had the job of

Celebrating Our Tenth Anniversary by ANNOUNCING THE OPENING of the Second Smith's Atlantic Service Station and Lake Park's New Hardware Store at 838 W. Fourth Street

cleaning the stairs and hallway to the apartments. Each week we had to sweep and mop the upstairs hallway and also sweep and mop the entrance and stairway to the apartments. I recently asked my brother, Bill, if he remembered what our pay was for

doing the cleaning. He said that he thought it was around $3 a week.

The entire building originally had an almost flat roof which meant, of course, frequent maintenance, especially to avoid leaks. That meant that usually every two or three years we would carry many five gallon buckets of roof tar and long handled brushes up the steps to the second floor hallway and then up an old wooden ladder through an opening above the hallway to the rooftop. Many times the "tar crew" consisted of Roscoe Harper, my brother, Bill, and me slopping and mopping tar during the hottest days of summer.

Obviously, the longest running business there has been Bossert's Hardware. After Sam Bossert's death I am pretty sure that one of his long time employees, Tom Bolger, ran the store for a while. After that, a Mr. Manbeck took over for several years and then, in 1980, "Young" Dan Pierce took the reins and is still there to this day.

The Dan Pierce Outdoor Shop got its start in 1976 when "Old" Dan Pierce and his wife began renovating the building after renting it from Dad. The Outdoor Shop was doing well, as was the hardware, so in early 1983, Dad and Mom agreed to sell the entire building to the Pierces. Sadly, Dad never got to see the many changes and renovations done by the Pierce family, as he died suddenly on June 6, 1983.

Originally, the Outdoor Shop was only in the large room between the hardware store and grocery store. Earl and Hazel Orner continued with the grocery store until Earl's birthday on July 4, 1986. At that time, the Orners were both in their mid 70s and they decided it was time to give up groceries, hoagies and penny candy to finally retire. It was after the Orners retired that the Pierces expanded the Outdoor Shop, which now included the original room plus the former grocery store. The Outdoor Shop is now in the hands of Dan's youngest son, Scott.

One of the sad notes to all of the memories from the early days is that nearly all of the men who helped in the construction of the building and the ones who went on to work for Dad over the years, are no longer with us. Dad died in 1983, Mom in 2007, and Earl Orner, who was so much a part of our family's life, passed away in 1991.

I recently found an old Royal Composition notebook that my mother, Mildred, used while doing all of the payroll records for Dad's businesses. This book covers the years 1948 to 1955. Besides being an amazing wife and mother, Mom was the only bookkeeper Dad ever had, and she kept meticulous records.

As I looked over the list of employees I realized that all of the guys that I personally knew are now deceased with the exception of James T. Hartland, who still lives in the "West End." Jim's first pay period with Dad was 69 years ago for the dates January 1 to 15, 1948. I have no idea what his hourly pay was or how many hours he worked, but his gross pay was $40. After deductions of 40 cents for Social Security, and $2.70 for income tax, his take home was a hearty $36.90. His top pay was in March and April of 1951, when he reached a gross bi-weekly pay of $96. The last payroll entry for Jim was from June 12 to 25, 1955. His wages were $85, with $1.70 off for Social Security, and a net of $83.30.

Dad's highest paid employees at the service stations were Earl Orner, who grossed $100 bi-weekly from 1948 through 1950, and Roy W. Penepacker, from McVeytown, who reached the lofty bi-weekly $100 level from late 1950 into 1951. Eugene Orner's top pay was $90 bi-weekly in 1949 and 1950.

C. SMITH OPENS A NEW STORE

Gasoline Service Station Owner to Manage Own Enterprise in Lake Park

Smith's Atlantic Service Station and Hardware Store, 838 West Fourth Street, was opened after more than a year of construction and preparation.

The store on the ground floor of a two story cement block and brick building measures 24 by 100 feet and will stock in addition to hardware, sporting goods and auto accessories.

The building has four apartments on the second floor which are not yet completed, but will be finished as soon as the necessary supplies can be procured.

Cloyd C. Smith, 508 West Fifth Street, owns the new business in addition to that of the Atlantic Service Station on West Market Street. The Market Street station will continue to be managed by Earl Orner and the station on Fourth Street will be managed by Eugene Orner. The hardware store will be run by Mr. Smith.

The service station section of the new business will be rebuilt in the spring and at that time adequate parking facilities will be made. A new lubrication system has been installed in the station.

Mr. Smith himself did a large part of the construction work on the new building.

Submitted by Carl Smith

A notice appeared in The Sentinel when Smith's Atlantic opened its West Fourth Street location.

"One of the sad notes to all of the memories from the early days is that nearly all of the men who helped in the construction of the building and the ones who went on to work for Dad over the years, are no longer with us. Dad died in 1983, Mom in 2007, and Earl Orner, who was so much a part of our family's life, passed away in 1991."

Shoop Radio and Television Repair

By the children of Robert F. Shoop Sr.:
Robert Shoop Jr., Lewistown
Mary Klingensmith, Reedsville
David Shoop, McClure
Barbara Barker, McVeytown

Robert F. Shoop Sr., began business in 1947, and turned in his business license 50 years to the day in March 1997. An article in the Lewistown Sentinel dated Oct. 12, 1948, (see next page) proclaimed the sixth game of the World Series was the first televised program of its kind in the borough of Lewistown.

Our father was in business from the beginning of television to the beginning of the throw away TV.

Robert Shoop began his training during the World War II as a radio networker in the Army Air Corps. After the war, he attended American Radio Institute in New York City on the GI bill.

H.P. Shoop, Robert's father, was an electrician supervisor at the American Viscose Corp., and encouraged him and taught him. That trait has carried on through the generations with sons and grandsons in the businesses.

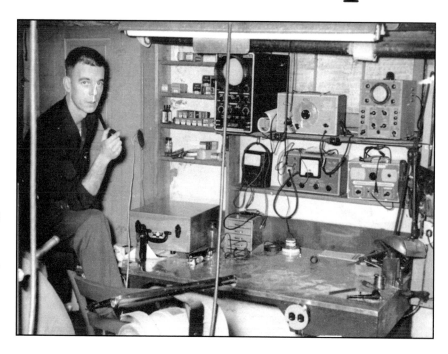

Robert Shoop Sr. is pictured in H. Percival Shoop's basement (his father), where he started his business in 1947. The photo was taken prior to 1954.

Photos submitted by
Mary Klingensmith

Robert Shoop used a 1956 Ford truck for service calls. This photo was taken in the early 1960s.

Robert Shoop moved his business to a new shop at the Rear of 602 South Grand Street, Lewistown. This photo was taken in 1964.

"... Our father was in business from the beginning of television to the beginning of the throw away TV ..."

10-12-48

6th Series Game First Televised Program to be Received in Boro

Television has come to town, intermittently clear and fluttery in its unpredictable infancy.

A small group, including newspaper and radio men, saw the last game of the current world series from a vantage point in the basement of the home of H. Percival Shoop, 602 South Grand Street.

The set, believed to be the first of its kind in the county is owned and operated by Robert M. Shoop, a local radio enthusiast who has been experimenting with television in his basement workshop for the past six weeks.

At lengthy intervals throughout the broadcast a concise picture of the player in different areas of the playing field could be seen on the 52-square inch screen.

Plainest of these were the shots at home plate when the most minute details of batter, catcher and umpire were visible.

When the pitchers wound up and pitched, it seemed the ball would continue on into the gadget-filled basement.

Close-up shots of runners going into bases were so real a splish of dirt thrown into the room off the tiny screen would not have been out of order.

When views of the huge crowd in the grandstands were shown the watchers had to stifle the impulse to reach out and purchase a sandwich from the vendor in the stands.

There were other times when the picture danced with a venetian blind effect or blanked out altogether. This was attributed in part to the overcast skies and the

(Continued on Page 12, Column 3)

TELEVISED GAME RECEIVED HERE

(Continued from First Page)

relays being made to bring television to this area.

The pictures were being relayed by micro-wave from Boston to New York, through Philadelphia to Baltimore on one channel and was picked up by a stratoliner, hovering 25,000 feet over Pittsburgh on another channel. It was being received within a radius of 250 miles of Pittsburgh.

Some of the interference was believed by Mr. Shoop to have come from the ignition on the plane while a humming undertone might have been the plane motors.

Several angles of the playing field were obtained by the use of a number of conveniently located cameras in the ball park.

Robert Shoop, who studied radio while with the Army Air Force and at the American Radio Institute in New York City, said today the only hope of consistent television in this area is by stratoliner because of the curvature of the earth.

Clipping from The Sentinel in 1948 submitted by Mary Klingensmith, Robert Shoop's daughter.

Then ...

Corkins Motor Inc.

By Tom Storm
Lewistown
(Information from Max Corkins)

Now ...

Corkins Motor Inc. was built by brothers Max, Bill and Glen Corkins, and their father, Harry, when the boys came home from World War II. Marker Construction was the contractor.

Kaiser Frazier was their first franchise, which they maintained for about two years. When Earl Beal gave up the Studebaker franchise on Electric Avenue to take on the Cadillac franchise, the Corkins' began selling Studebakers. This dealership lasted until 1953, at which time they opened a used car lot across the street.

After being rented out as a furniture store for a few years, it was remodeled as a bowling alley by Bill and Glen Corkins in 1958, under the name DeCor Lanes.

Today, under the name Lewistown Lanes, it is still operated as a bowling alley, under different ownership.

The aerial photo was taken in the early 1950s.

Interestingly, the building directly across West Fourth Street from Corkins, which now houses Sky View Video, was originally built to house a Tucker Automobile dealership.

The Keystone Motor Co.

Sentinel archives

The Keystone Motor Co. garage was located at 12-20 West Third Street, Lewistown. Later it was Novak Motors, a Plymouth/Dodge dealer. The building contained a roller skating rink upstairs. The photo was taken pre-1920. The site of this building is now a municipal parking lot adjacent to the United Fire Company. A photo of the building was submitted for publication by Tom Storm, of Lewistown. The same image, above, came from an advertisement for the company published in 1925, and is used here because the quality was better for reproduction. The ad states that the business was established in 1914. Signs say: Willys-Overland Fine Motor Car; Packard, White, Garford, Reo Trucks.

'Bobby Campbell's Diner'

By D.J. McCrory
Lewistown

I found this old clipping while cleaning my attic. It belonged to my brother, Lee Sanchez. We knew it as Bobby Campbell's diner.

The caption under the photo says:
YE OLDE EDITOR'S SCRAP-BOOK — Here's another interesting photo of the trolley car that was converted to a diner and which today is known as Campbell's Diner. It was taken in the mid-1930s by Kepler Studio. The menu underneath the window lists the following prices: Yankee bean soup, 10 cents; vegetable soup, 10 cents; roast fresh ham, 45 cents; pork chop, 40 cents; boiled ham and cabbage, 40 cents; roast sirloin of beef, 40 cents; and pork and beans, 35 cents. Sign on the door reads: "Thirsty? Just ... demand the genuine WHISTLE." The photo was presented for publication [in the County Observer weekly newspaper, date unknown] by Anne Fisher.

Leoras was 'the' place to stop in Lewistown

Bill Logan

A brief history of Leoras Cafeteria based on newspaper clippings submitted by Bill and Pam Logan, of Lewistown

People of one generation may remember Leoras as "the" place to stop after Saturday night dances at the YMCA in the 1940s and '50s. Others may remember the guys in Lewistown's unofficial "Breakfast Club," who spent their early morning hours before work gabbing about their days, sports and the latest headlines.

Many, many more remember the homemade meals and pies that sustained the hungry in downtown Lewistown for well over 50 years.

Bill Logan and his wife, Pam, were associated with Leoras for many of those years.

The business was started in 1947, by Steve and Phoebe Leoras, Bill's aunt and uncle.

Steve came home from the war in the 1940s, and moved to Lewistown from Altoona with his wife, Phoebe. Phoebe was the sister of Bill's mother.

Steve had been working as a cook in the Army, and Bill's father owned a couple buildings on Dorcas Street, so Steve opened a restaurant at 28 South Dorcas Street.

Bill says the original Leoras Restaurant opened on Groundhog Day in 1947.

A few years later, they expanded next door with a dining room, and later added upstairs banquet facilities.

The restaurant operated at that location until 1968, when it was taken for downtown redevelopment, razed and the space became a parking lot. A few months later, the Leoras found

Photos submitted by Bill and Pam Logan

Interior of Leoras when it was located on South Dorcas Street

Photos submitted by Bill and Pam Logan

Leoras was located on South Dorcas Street ...

... until it relocated to the lower level of 19 South Brown Street in 1968. Bill Logan stands front of the cafeteria's counter in 1984.

new quarters at 19 South Brown Street, and re-opened the restaurant as a cafeteria in August 1968.

Bill Logan, and his wife, Pam, purchased the business from his aunt and uncle in 1977. He said he practically grew up in the restaurant, as Steve and Phoebe were like his second parents.

When it came time, the transfer of ownership "came natural." Bill and Pam left their jobs as schoolteachers to work as full-time owners-managers in the cafeteria.

Two years later, the Logans purchased the building in which the cafeteria occupied the lower level.

Phoebe Leoras stayed on, in charge of baking pies that were legendary in downtown Lewistown cuisine.

The business was open for breakfast and lunch every day except Sunday, and sometimes on Wednesday and Friday evenings, also serving banquets during hours in which they were closed to the public.

Bill and Pam's extensive collection of newspaper clippings about their business includes a 1987 story snipped from the Philadelphia Inquirer, as well as an article that appeared in "Pennsylvania Farmer" in 1984.

The Inquirer article, "Good-luck Goose Day," explained the central Pennsylvania observance of Michaelmas Day on Sept. 29, in which "everybody feasts on the fowl."

Phoebe Leoras, seated, and Pam and Bill Logan, 1997

Pam Logan, a 1984 Mystery Tipper winner

The story quotes Bill Logan: "Last year I served about 260 goose dinners. Goose Day is our biggest day of the year. I compare it with Mother's Day. Goose is our only special that day, and about 99 percent of the customers will have it."

Goose Day dinners had been served at Leoras since 1947, when Bill's uncle opened the restaurant.

The article in "Pennsylvania Farmer" focused on Pam, who, in 1984, was the Mifflin County Dairy Promotion Council's first winner in the "Mystery Tipper" contest. In the

promotion, the council selected a local personality to award $5 tips to waiters or waitresses who suggest milk to their customers. Mystery Tipper Charles E. "Yogi" Laub, the Mifflin County Registrar of Wills and Recorder of Deeds, awarded his $5 check to Pam after she asked him if he would like to have a glass of milk with the sandwich she was preparing for his lunch.

Bill and Pam sold Leoras on Sept. 6, 2001, and, after changing hands a couple times, the business closed for good in 2006.

Prestie M. Headings: Druggist

Information compiled from newspaper clippings submitted by Judy Headings, of Yeagertown, whose late husband, Prestie M. (Chip) Headings III, was the druggist's grandson.

Prestie M. Headings Sr. Druggist

The pharmacist who can make and hold a commanding position in the exacting profession must have ability and talent of a very high order, for in no branch of professional life are the requirements so exacting, and various years of experience and study are the prime essentials of the successful druggist.

One of the distinguished members of the profession was Prestie M. Headings, first located at 147 East Market Street, in a business established January 1, 1904.

The store was handsomely fitted up with walnut trimmings. A complete stock of pure drugs and proprietary medicines, toilet and fancy articles, cigars, candies, etc., all of acknowledged merit and purity, was carried.

A specialty was made of compounding doctors' prescriptions from absolutely pure ingredients by reliable assistants.

A beautiful soda fountain was installed, where only pure fruit syrups were ever used.

A complete stock of perfumes, toilet soaps, hair brushes, sponges, etc., were kept in stock.

Prestie Milroy Headings, son of Isaac and Maria (Metz) Headings, was born on the farm near Honey Creek station in Mifflin County, Pennsylvania, on October 19, 1876.

He was educated in the public schools of Milroy, graduating from Milroy High School and Millersville State Normal. He taught school in New Lancaster Valley for two years after leaving the Normal School.

He married, in June 1900, Estella Hayes, born in Pittsburgh, Pennsylva-

Photos for this feature courtesy Judy Headings, Sentinel archives and Mifflin County Historical Society

nia, daughter of L. O. Hayes, a retired coal dealer, of Pittsburgh. Both he and his wife were members of the Lutheran church.

Headings then entered Philadelphia College of Pharmacy, from which he graduated 1901. After receiving his diploma, he was employed as a registered pharmacist in the drugstore of H. M. Andress, at Homestead, Pennsylvania, for two years, and for the succeeding two years occupied the same position with A. C. Hyde, at New Castle, Pennsylvania.

On January 1, 1905, Mr. Headings purchased from the heirs, the drugstore of G. C. Dippery, in the Harris Block, on East Market Street, Lewistown, and for two years conducted a successful drug business at that location.

He then moved to the Will Lind building, later owned by the Methodist Episcopal Church, remain-

The second location of the Headings Drugstore was at the corner of Dorcas and Valley streets at the Five Points, across the street from the store's final location, on the lot which is now known as Fountain Square.

ing there four years. The Fretz Funeral Home, then the Heller & Baudoux Funeral Home later located there.

He then purchased from A. C. Mayes, a store at Valley and Chestnut streets, also known as the Five Points, or Fountain Square, where he had a handsomely equipped, well-stocked and well-patronized store, with a varied line of cut glass, china, drugs, confectionery, fine stationery, fountain — in short, a modern drugstore.

A landmark to both old and young, the store has always been a mecca for the youth of the community, and the welcome mat was always out for school pupils, a representative portion of the citizenry of which Dr. Headings

Five Points
Lewistown

was always especially fond.

The store, once referred to as one of the largest pharmacies between Philadelphia and Pittsburgh, always bore a metropolitan air, and was stocked from top to bottom with everything conceivable to the drug business.

Dr. Headings was president of the YMCA board of directors for 16 years, until he declined the post in 1946. He was then made president emeritus and continued as a member of the board.

He presented an outright gift of 7.37 acres of land to the Dickson-YMCA Field in August of 1940, purchasing the land for that purpose.

Deeply interested in public and religious education, he served the Lewistown school district as a member of the board for 14 years, including 12 as its president.

He gave his hearty support to the erection of the Lewistown Junior High School when this program was launched in 1925, and was one of the founders of the Mifflin County Child Welfare Services and the Lewistown Housing and Development Company, serving both as a director. He was chairman of the Mifflin County Crippled Children's Association for many years.

The Headings name can be seen on Chestnut Street side of the drugstore building at Five Points, Lewistown.

Headings was also involved in the American Druggists Syndicate, a wholesale manufacturing and jobbing drug association. He was a Democrat in politics, a member of the Masonic order, and of the Independent Order of Odd Fellows.

Tragedy entered Headings' busy life when he was attacked and brutally beaten in his drugstore as he was closing on Sunday evening, August 5, 1945. As a result of this, he lay for many weeks at the

A look inside the store - 1929

point of death. His son, Prestie M. Headings Jr., returned from military service to run the store while his father recovered, although he never regained full health. His brother, Lewis Headings, also operated a drugstore in downtown Lewistown, in the Wollner building on Monument Square.

Prestie M. Headings Sr. died of coronary occlusion at his home at 387 South Main Street, Lewistown, at 12:10 a.m. on Sunday, March 5, 1950.

Prestie Jr. also became a pharmacist and operated his father's drugstore until closing it around 1970.

In 2009, his late son, Prestie M. (Chip) Headings III, recalled: "I have many fond memories of helping my dad in the drugstore. I washed windows, ran errands to my uncle's (Lew Headings) drugstore at the square, and delivered medicine to people at their homes.

"But the best part was sneaking ice cream sundaes from the soda fountain!"

Prestie M.
Headings Jr.

Irene Shimp worked behind the counter at Headings Drugstore at Five Points. The date of this photo is unknown.

MAN, WOMAN SOUGHT AFTER ATTACK ON LOCAL DRUGGIST

Submitted by Judy Headings
Yeagertown

(Reprinted from The Sentinel, Aug. 5, 1945)

DR. HEADINGS BEATEN, BOUND IN ATTEMPTED STORE HOLD-UP

Couple accosted as they leave store by neighbors aroused by sounds of scuffle

VICTIM REPORTED IN CRITICAL CONDITION

Police Learn Suspected Pair Had Been in Community Three Days; Boro Officer's Car Stolen

Attacked and brutally beaten in his drug store at the corner of Valley and Chestnut streets as he was closing the place about 10 o'clock Sunday night, Dr. P.M. Headings is in serious condition in Lewistown Hospital.

He suffered a severe gash across the top of his head nearly from temple to temple, both eyes are closed from a blow on the nose, and his neck and jaws are swollen and black and blue

PRESTIE M. HEADINGS

Druggist.

Submitted by Judy Headings

Prestie M. Headings Sr.

from being beaten by a man and a woman, both described "about 30."

Hospital attendants said that his condition was serious because of his age but that he had slept several hours during the night. This morning he was lucid at intervals, but up to noon today was still in a condition that police could not question him for some badly needed information.

Surgeons told members of the family that he may have suffered a concussion, but that it would be "a day or two before it can be determined definitely."

A man and a woman, whose

descriptions police have broadcast, were the objects of one of the sternest manhunts in recent years in this community.

They are definitely connected with the aggravated assault and battery and the attempted robbery, and were described accurately by a half dozen persons who served them at the soda counter and who saw them leave the store after the attack.

The attack and attempted robbery were discovered by Mrs. Fern Miller and her daughter, Helen Mae Miller, and the latter's friend, Edward A. Welsh, 125 West Fourth Street.

According to the story related by Mrs. Miller, the three were sitting on the rear roof of the apartment building over the Headings drug store about 10 o'clock when they heard voices and the crash of glass in the prescription room of the store below.

The three found the druggist lying on his face in a pool of blood in the prescription room with his wrists bound behind him, and with the room a shambles.

The first crash was followed by two more. Mrs. Miller said that she remarked to her daughter and Mr. Welsh, "Something's happened to Mr. Headings."

She said that they got up from deck chairs and a swing in which they had been sitting and walked across the planks over the roof to a rear window where they made ineffectual attempts to see into the prescription room.

"I heard Mr. Headings groan 'Oh, Oh,' several times and then the three of us ran down the steps intending to go in the store and see what the trouble was.

"The noise of us walking across the planks and running down the stairs must have scared them away. As we got to the door the store was dark except for a small light in the front window and a small light in the prescription room.

"Just as we got to the door, the man and woman stepped out and pulled the door shut. My daughter asked if Mr. Headings was in there and the man replied, 'He's out.'

"I stepped aside as they stepped down from the doorway and the man put his hand up to push back his long blond hair. I said to him: 'You did something to Mr. Headings.'

"With that, the man and woman took to their heels and sped down Chestnut Street and made a turn into the alley near the Weis Store.

"We went in the store and found Mr. Headings in a pool of blood in the prescription room. I called to him several times, and the third time he answered," Mrs. Miller related.

While Mrs. Miller attempted to untie the blood-covered and slippery rawhide that bound the druggist's wrists behind him, Mr. Welsh telephoned to the police department, while Mrs. Miller's daughter ran out and asked several people sit-

Headings Drugstore building at Five Points, Lewistown

ting in a car on Valley Street to take her to the police station.

Mrs. Miller, in the meantime, screamed for help and attempted to get the druggist away from the pool of blood that was threatening to smother him.

Abe Colabine, night deskman at the police station, said that the telephone call reached the police office at 10:10 p.m. and he immediately sent a call to the police car.

Harry W. Jacobs, meanwhile, received the call at Juniata and West Fourth streets while cruising along and sped to the store. He said that he advised the druggist to lie still on the floor as he made efforts to rise when he reached there, and within minutes the Fame Fire Company ambulance arrived and took the injured man to the hospital.

Matthew Soccio, who conducts the shoe shine business

on Chestnut Street near Dorcas Street and was open at the time, rushed to the scene and summoned the ambulance.

Dr. Lewis E. Headings, son of the victim, was out of town when the tragedy occurred. He arrived here today and went to the hospital to see his seriously ill father. The son took charge of the store business today.

When the attack was discovered and the druggist removed to the hospital, police reached G. McCrea Miller, a druggist employed by Lewis Headings in his Monument Square store. Mr. Miller reached the store and remained there until 4:15 o'clock this morning, when police finished fingerprinting and photographing signs of the struggle.

Chief of Police H.O. Landis was notified immediately and he, in turn, asked the assistance of State Police.

Within a matter of minutes, all of the available borough

policemen, including Chief Landis, Sergeant Elwood Albert, who was off duty for the night, Policeman Jacobs and Jay Rhodes reached the scene.

They were followed by State Troopers Edward P. Rowan and A.A. Verbitski, who, with Chief Landis, pushed the investigation at the store.

Meanwhile, Troopers A.C. Murafka, John M. Amick, Clyde Smith and George Finkebiner, along with Borough Policemen Jacobs and Rhodes, started a search of local streets and highways for a couple described as follows:

Man: About 30 years of age, long blond hair, fair complexion, 5 feet, 7 inches tall, 150 pounds, slender build, wearing a blue shirt and dark trousers. His sleeves are either short or rolled up and on his left arm are several adhesive tape patches.

Woman: Aged about 30 years, brunette with long black or brown hair with a long bob, a red flower in her hair, 5 feet 4 inches tall, and wearing a white blouse and a black skirt.

While borough police were staging a dragnet, an alarm was sent out to State Police barracks in Duncannon, Huntingdon, Pleasant Gap and Selinsgrove to have the entire area sealed off.

While the officers were outside checking hotels, rooming houses and cabins all through this area on the hunt for the couple, Troopers Rowan, Verbitski and Chief Landis were trying to reconstruct the crime and were consulting store employees.

From employees of the store, the officers learned that the man visited the store at least on one occasion last week at the soda bar, and was in the store earlier Sunday evening.

Shirley Carstetter of 15 Logan Street, and Marilyn Carstetter of 25 Helen Street, were in the store when the couple came in sometime before 11 o'clock and sat on the stools near the door, at the soda fountain.

Shirley said that the woman ordered a double Coca-Cola and the man a chocolate milkshake. The woman asked Shirley if Betty Carstetter was her sister, that she had met her in Baltimore and at Ambrosia Inn.

Shortly afterwards the two girls left and the druggist began preparations to close.

As police reconstruct it, he pulled down the shade of the Chestnut Street entrance and then went to the Valley Street door and pulled the shade there.

It was then that the two are believed to have made their original attack upon him. When police entered the scene, they found the druggist's white Panama hat about 15 feet from the door and his glasses three feet away on the other side of the aisle leading back to the prescription room.

Marks on the floor indicated that he was either dragged or pushed by force to the back room where police believe that efforts were made to force him to open the safe.

A pound jar of cold cream was smashed over his head,

DR. HEADINGS

P. M. HEADINGS DIES AT HOME

Pharmacist, Long a Civic Leader, Expires Saturday Midnight of Heart Attack

Dr. Prestie M. Headings, Lewistown druggist for nearly a half century, and prominent as member and head of many service, civic and religious organizations, died of coronary occlusion at his home, 387 South Main Street, at 12:10 A. M. on Sunday.

A graduate of Milroy High School, Dr. Headings taught school in New Lancaster Valley for two years prior to his graduation from the Philadelphia College of Pharmacy in 1901.

The Headings drug store was first located on East Market Street between Brown and Dorcas Streets. Later it was located on Fountain Square at the site now occupied by the Fretz Funeral Home. Finally Dr. Headings purchased the property at the corner of Valley and Chestnut Streets and moved his business to this spot where it has remained.

1950

cutting a gash in his scalp, and he either was hit with a pint bottle of lime water, or he knocked it over in the struggle.

Cold cream and blood covered the druggist's head and face, and chunks of the stuff were scattered about the room.

Another Headings Drugstore

The following is an excerpt from an article written in 2008 by Forest K. Fisher, of the Mifflin County Historical Society, for a series published in The Sentinel about historically significant buildings in Mifflin County. The drugstore owned by Lewis Headings was one of the many businesses that were at one time located in what is known, historically, as the Wollner building, on Monument Square in Lewistown.

Over the past 100 years, the Wollner building has had numerous tenants in addition to the Trust Company. Certainly one of the most memorable, in the minds of many, was the drugstore of Lewis H. Headings Sr. The druggist was affectionately known to all who frequented his store as "Lew." The Headings Drug Company occupied the main storeroom at 16 West Market Street for more than 30 years, continuing in the tradition of his father, pharmacist P. M. Headings. An ad for L. H. Headings Drug Store in the Friday, May 28, 1943, edition of the Sentinel notes his store in the Wollner building. The advertisement urged, "See our selection of Hall-Mark Greeting Cards for all occasions." Along with Headings' companion store at Five Points, the business was a Lewistown institution for over a generation until his retirement in 1973.

Photos courtesy of the Mifflin County Historical Society

The Wollner building on Monument Square has housed many businesses, including the Pallas Restaurant from 1926 to 1939, and later Lewis Headings Drugstore.

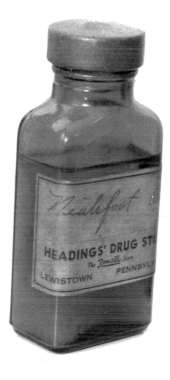

Memorabilia from Headings Drugstores

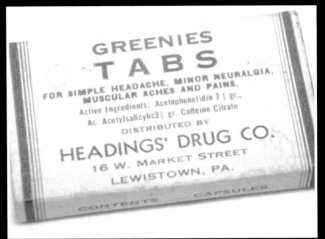

Medicine box and bottles from Headings Drugstore, as well as Dr. C.K. Young and Son, of McClure, are from the the collection of Randy Cutshall, of Lewistown.

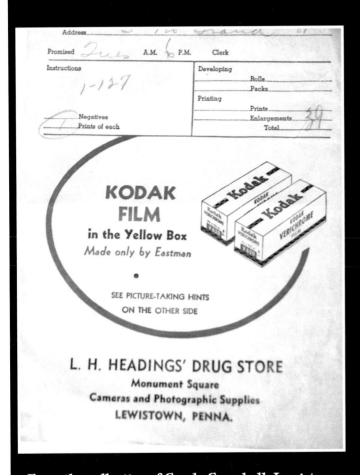

From the collection of Carole Campbell, Lewistown

Relics from both Headings' drugstores are now the property of Lewis H. "Buck" Headings Jr.

Photo courtesy of the Mifflin County Historical Society

Mike's Insulation Service

By Mary Lou Sigler
Reedsville

In 1965, at the age of 43, my dad, Michael J. Porpotage, decided to take a chance and open his own business. Having worked in various jobs before and after his tour of duty, Thunderbolt Across Europe, with the U.S. Army during WWII, Dad established Mike's Insulation Service. In an effort to save people money on heating and cooling costs, Dad learned as much as he could about various types of insulation and decided to offer what he considered the best. The business swiftly grew beyond insulation to electrical service, installing windows, plumbing, roofing, siding, and general remodeling. With my mother as secretary and bookkeeper, Dad was finally able to make a living without facing layoffs such as he had experienced throughout the years after WWII.

While Dad had various employees during the 22 years that he owned and operated Mike's Insulation Service, his most loyal and most dedicated employee was no doubt my brother Joe, who in 1987 became the owner of the business. At a very young age, during the summer months, Joe would hide on Dad's step van so that he could "go to work" with Dad. Dad would have to stop at a pay phone – no cellphones in those days – and call Mom so that she would not worry about where Joe was. Joe loved being with Dad. And when Dad become ill with a serious heart condition leading to Joe's ownership of the business, Dad insisted on "going to work" with Joe because he loved being a part of the business even if he could no longer do as much physical labor. Dad and Joe seemed inseparable during the work day for many years.

In addition to originating their own jobs and growing the business, they also worked as subcontractors for Robert S. Palm, a well-known local

Photo submitted by Mary Lou Sigler

Michael J. Porpotage, right, and son, Joe, are pictured in the late 1970s or early '80s.

contractor, and for another contractor in the State College area. In recent years, Mr. Palm's son, Steve, let me know that his dad very much respected my dad and brother. According to Steve, his dad trusted and knew he could depend on Mike's Insulation Service to complete jobs well and in a timely manner. Of course, the respect and appreciation were mutual. My dad always spoke highly of Robert Palm.

Dad and Joe loved working for people and always wanted to ensure excellent customer service. Often, on weekends or in the evening, when someone called with an emergency, Dad or Joe would answer the call. They refused to say "no" to someone whose family needed electricity re-

stored or plumbing repaired.

I chose to write this article about my dad's business because I was always very proud of my dad and the fact that he not only had the courage to open his own business as a middle-aged man, but also was well-liked and admired as an honest, hard-working businessman with a sense of humor

Photo submitted by Mary Lou Sigler

Joe Porpotage is on Mike's Insulation Service's step van, while the original truck is at the left.

and a great personality. Even after 25 years since my dad's death, people continue to tell me how much they respected my dad because he truly cared about doing his work well and pleasing his customers.

Likewise, I often hear very similar compliments regarding my brother Joe, who, perhaps, was even more of a perfectionist about his work than my dad but also had a quite a sense of humor. After an electrical service installation was completed, an inspector had to certify that the job met all standards. One of the inspectors who is now deceased often told Joe that, even without checking, he knew that Joe's work would be flawless.

Knowing that Dad and Joe were appreciated and trusted to do their work with accuracy and precision continues to make me proud although Mike's Insulation Service closed in 1994.

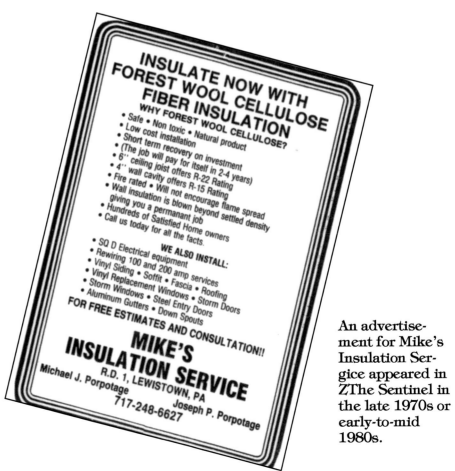

An advertisement for Mike's Insulation Service appeared in ZThe Sentinel in the late 1970s or early-to-mid 1980s.

Elsesser's Produce

By Vickie Elsesser-Vu
Mechanicsville, Maryland

Henry C. Elsesser was the initial owner/operator of Elsesser's Potatoes.

On July 10, 1944, when World War II was in full swing, Henry was severely injured in a truck accident when he went to get a load of potatoes and apples on the Eastern Shore. More than 50 percent of his body was burned in the following explosion at this accident.

His son, Samuel Elsesser, was serving in Korea with the U.S. Army at the time. He was discharged for humanitarian reasons to come back to Lewistown, Pennsylvania, to manage the family business during his father's recovery period in the burn unit.

Eventually, Samuel and his older brother, Harold, bought the businesses from their father. In the 1960s, they expanded it to sell produce, too. They tried to establish regular business hours for opening and closing, instead of waiting for the cars to pull in or the car lights to notify them that a customer was there. Both men's wives, Alma and Phyllis, respectively, helped to wait on customers and manage the books for the business.

In 1965, Harold and Phyllis moved to Florida to buy a motel, and Samuel bought him out. Alma stepped up to help Samuel even more by making fruit baskets during the holidays, as well as her and Phyllis' previous jobs. She also lent her artistic talents to decorating the trucks with cartoon characters. By then, there were a fleet of trucks with regular routes to local businesses for their wholesale produce needs and resale to the public. Alma was also responsible for the company

logo ... "Serving Those Who Want the Best."

Samuel and Alma bought the lot on the other side of the warehouse, and built their home so they could be available to wait on customers, since it seemed difficult to establish regular business hours. It was not unusual for the truck drivers to pop in for a cup of coffee.

Customers would come to the "warehouse" for their potatoes and produce. The warehouse, which was located directly behind Henry's house on Lewistown Heights, consisted of a large storage area where the potatoes were stacked in 50-pound bags. Up a few steps to the "showroom" was where the fruits and vegetables were displayed for retail sale. There was an old-fashioned cash register, and two large walk-in refrigerated rooms. A docking station was in the rear of the building, where the trucks would load and unload for their deliveries.

In the basement, there was a "pecking" machine. Fifty-pound bags of potatoes were dumped in the one end and the conveyor belt would move them along, where they were automatically divided, tied shut with metal clasps, caught and stacked — waiting for distribution. Henry or Samuel would usually be at the top of the conveyor belt to pick out the rotten ones, or the extra-large ones for Hartley's Potato Chips (another famous local business).

On Sunday nights, the telephone

call to the broker was placed so that the week's produce would be ordered. A tractor trailer would then be dispatched to the docks on the south side of Philadelphia to stock the warehouse. Of course, there were also random deliveries by trucks with special loads: peaches, apples or watermelons. It was not unusual to be included in a watermelon line — passing the fruit off the trucks and onto the warehouse one by one.

The business was sold in 1979, when Samuel went on to start a janitorial service, which eventually led to Lewistown Paper Co., where Mark Elsesser, his son, bought him out and is currently located in Burnham.

A whopping 25 cents could be earned to help with the pecking of potatoes — for a whole morning's work. Other memories include picking tomatoes or selling corn on the cob in our wagons for 50 cents a dozen. Awh ... the smell of rotten tomatoes beings back such sweet memories.

• • •

Vickie Elsesser-Vu is Samuel Elsesser's daughter, and Mark Elsesser's sister.

THE LOG CABIN INN
G. F. Smith, Proprietor
MENU

SANDWICHES		DINNERS		HOT DRINKS	
Lettuce	.10	Steak	.85	Coffee	.05
Hamburg	.15	Small Steak	.65	Tea	.10
Cheese	.15	Pork Chops	.65	Chocolate	.10
Baked Ham	.15	Choice of Two Vegetables, Dessert and Coffee with all Dinners.			
Roast Pork	.15			Soft Drinks	.05 and .10
Pork and		Fried Shrimp	.50		

The Log Cabin Inn

By Nancy Bogar McClure

My dad built the Log Cabin Inn in 1930. I was 2 weeks old when Mom, Dad and my sisters, Phyllis and Shirley, moved in. They used to say that the "super" on the project made 25 cents an hour.

It was basically a restaurant in the beginning. See the prices on the menu. It was later like a nightclub. The bands were hired by the month, I think. They lived in the area during their engagement. Some put on stage shows.

It seemed like the place to go to in the 1930s and 1940s. Some people were there every night — some to dance and some to just visit with friends.

After the war, we were so busy we had to add more parking lots. I was old enough then to work there. I sat in the kitchen at a little opening and took care of the waitress' orders and made change.

In the early days, the bartenders and waitresses wore uniforms. It was exciting when the "Angelica" book came to order new "wear."

Mom passed away in 1950. Dad sold the Log Cabin Inn in 1962, and built a little house on the hill on Snook Road. He passed away in 1999, a month short of turning 99. Shirley passed away in 2002, and Phyllis lives at William Penn at age 96.

Rye Sour					
The Hurric...					.35
Ward Eigh...					.35
Whiskey Collins	.35	**RUM BASE**		Bamboo Cocktail	.25
Log Cabin De Luxe	.35	Rum	.15 to .25	Port Wine Cocktail	.25
		Rum Highball	.25		
GIN BASE		Rum Rickey	.25	**WINES**	
Gin	.10 to .15	Daiquiri	.35	Muscatel	.20
Gin Rickey	.25	Rum Collins	.35	Port	.20
Tom Collins	.30	Rum Daisy	.35	Sherry	.20
John Collins	.30			Tokay	.20
Log Cabin De Luxe	.30	**BRANDY BASE**			
Pink Lady	.35	Brandy	.15	Domestic Champagne	$1.15
Gin Fizz	.35	Cold Deck	.35	(Per Bottle)	
Martini	.35	Harvard	.35	**BEER**	
Michell's Brew	.35	Sidecar	.35	Glass	.10
Haney's Punch	.35	Cuban	.35	Pitcher	.65

THE LOG CABIN INN
G. F. Smith, Proprietor
MENU

A postcard from 1939, with a one cent stamp, shows The Horton Orchestra and Revue, which Nancy Bogar describes as "a mother, father and four daughters band and night club act. The youngest girl went to school with me when they were here."

Photos submitted by Nancy Bogar

G.F. Smith built the Log Cabin Inn in 1930.

The men who built the Log Cabin Inn, 1930.

Nancy Bogar's aunt, Dot Wray Barnett, a waitress, (note the uniform), Phyllis, Shirley and Nancy, 1932.

THE LOG CABIN INN
G. F. Smith, Proprietor
MENU

Remembering Lewistown, Burnham

Editor's note: This article originally appeared in "Juniata Valley 2009: I Remember When," a special section published by The Sentinel in 2009.

By Connie Leonard
Lewistown

Here are some memories of the Lewistown and Burnham areas from a local "baby boomer." This is the way I remember these things from the '50s and '60s; some of you may remember the names and more precise locations.

I remember when ...
• We lived on Freedom Avenue and the ice cream truck came by every Saturday evening. We all got a 10-cent cone of our favorite flavor (either vanilla or chocolate).
• The local bus (green and white) would pick us up on a street corner to take us to downtown Lewistown to shop. In those days, downtown Lewistown was "THE" place to shop! Shopping centers weren't in existence in the area yet.
• Woolworth's 5&10 was on Market Street and had creaky wooden floors.
• McMeens and Danks were "THE" stores to shop in. ("THE" meaning prestigious.)
• Murphy's 5&10 was on the square. I remember the big paper mache stork in the babies department. The candy department had glass cases full of "yummy" looking candy and you ordered by the pound, which was put in little brown paper bags. I liked the magazine rack where my beloved Katie Keen "funny books" were found. At Christmas time, Santa sat in a corner of the basement and when you sat on his lap and told him what you wanted for Christmas, you got a free goldfish in a little clear bag with water in. Mom wasn't very happy with that one because then you had to buy a fish bowl and fish food (wasn't that clever merchandising?)
• McCrory's 5&10 was just up the street from Murphy's. It, like Woolworth's, had creaky wooden floors. I remember how they had peepees at Easter time that were in pastel colored dye (we found out later that the dye was actually harmful for the birds). I had begged for one and got a white one to take home. He was my pet until he disappeared one day. Later I found out we ate him one evening for supper! I felt weird knowing that I ate my pet, but I never knew exactly when he "graced" our table.
• The Burnham Drive-In was where the J.C. Penney shopping center is now. I remember playing on the swings by the screen right before watching the "Bride of Frankenstein." My sister and her "then boyfriend" (now husband) took his sister and me. I remember my mother

Photo submitted by Connie Leonard

Spigie's Esso was on the corner of South Main Street and Green Avenue in Lewistown.

growling at my sister for taking me to see that since my mother and I had a few "sleepless" nights from dreaming of Frankenstein.
• Long's Dairy was where the Burnham OIP is now. Both my sisters worked there as teens. They had good ice cream.
• Rushing home from a Sunday drive to watch "Lassie" on TV.
• Saturday evenings watching Lawrence Welk.
• TV programs such as .. "Leave It To Beaver," "Have Gun Will Travel," "The Rebel," "Ed Sullivan," "The Twilight Zone," "Sky King," "The Outer Limits" ...
• Going to the Newtown Firehouse every Christmas morning for a popcorn ball and a bag of Hershey miniatures.
• Lewistown's Christmas parade on a Saturday morning before Christmas and Santa was always the last float.
• The Blue Goose Restaurant on the corner of South Main and Charles streets.
• The old Lewistown High School, which had a cafeteria that was originally meant to be a swimming pool, and a shaky balcony in the auditorium.
• My sister was in the first class to graduate from the new Chief Logan High School in 1960 (that combined Yeagertown and Burnham high schools).
• The Dairy Belle was in the building across from Dr.

A Look Back: Businesses in the Juniata Valley

The Montgomery Ward store on square in downtown Lewistown, 1950s

Patel's office (which wasn't there then) on Logan Boulevard.

• Pleasant Acres East was preceded by a pond that we ice skated on in the '50s.

• The milkman left glass quarts of milk in an aluminum box on your porch and when it was cold, the cream rose to the top, pushing the little cardboard stopper out of the bottle.

• We also had a "bread man" who delivered bread and baked goods to our house.

• Selling Beaver's Bakery doughnuts for a school project at Burnham Elementary.

• Going to the Burnham "Y" to eat lunch during school because Burnham Elementary didn't have a cafeteria yet.

• Hambright's Hardware on Freedom Avenue (my father went to grade school in that building in the '30s).

• Ushers to seat you and make kids "behave" at the Miller The-ater, which was one big theater.

• Sitting in the balcony of the Embassy Theater and throwing popcorn down at the people below.

• Seeing the first Beatles movie at the Embassy and screaming (it was the thing to do then).

• Seeing a kids' movie at the Rialto on the Square in Lewistown.

• Montgomery Ward store on the Square, with three floors in which to shop.

• Dianne Candy Shop.

• Rea & Derrick's drug store and snack bar, where kids gathered after school.

• Dianne and Artley women's apparel shops on Market Street.

• A millinery (hat) shop on Chestnut Street ... don't remember the name of it.

• Berney's Toy Shop.

• Ruhl's Men's Shop.

• Saturday morning shopping downtown with curlers in your hair meant you had a date that night!

• Hoagies at Murphy's 5&10 were three for a dollar!

• Spigies Produce on Logan Boulevard.

• Spigie's Esso on the corner of South Main Street and Green Avenue.

• Lewistown high school girls wore wool shorts and knee socks to all football games regardless of how cold or hot it was!

• Nothing but fields existed beyond the 900 block of Sixth Street in Lewistown (McCoy Manor and Goss Terrace didn't exist then).

• The Lewistown bowling lanes were across the Stevens' Motel.

• Kish Park pool had rides (roller coaster, bumper cars, tractors, swings, merry-go-round, boats, "Fun in the Dark," miniature golf , which still exists, and skeeball).

• Splash hops at either Kish pool or Burnham pool.

• Hops at the Burnham Y!

I hope this jarred some pleasant memories for you.

Memories were made at Harry's

By Ida M. Fowler
Lewistown

I worked at Harry's Market from 1975 to 1990. The most wonderful memories I have are of the wonderful people who came through the doors every day. They became like a family to us. We cried with them and laughed with them. Even today I meet people who say, "I know you from Harry's."

We had candy fish and lollipops, which Harry gave to the children. Harry got a soda fountain. We had a little boy come in and crawl up on Harry's lap. He would say, "I awful firsty," and Harry would give him a drink.

I have so many wonderful memories. Cora Hunter worked for Harry for years. Everyone loved her and she became my adopted mother. They used to call her "Red," because of her hair.

We had a man who came in every few weeks and order a pound of "sawdust." That was a pound of

Photo courtesy Mifflin County Historical Society
Harry's Fruit Market, Burnham

dried beef chipped so that it looked like sawdust.

I used to go in early in the morning and the guys on their way to work would stop for coffee or a sandwich for their lunch.

I am so proud to have been a part of Harry's Market. Harry is no longer with us, but the memories linger on.

I was married to Harry for 22 years. He went home to heaven March 17, 2013, after a long battle with cancer.

"HAPPY BIRTHDAY" FROM RED BARN™

We have a great birthday gift for you. Just bring this card to the Red Barn Restaurant, and we will give you a FREE Birthday Dinner — a pure-beef Red Barn Hamburger, French Fries, and a big Milk Shake. Just because this is *your* day.

112 Electric Avenue
Lewistown, Pennsylvania

'When the hungries hit ...

Randy Cutshall, of Lewistown, purchased this birthday card from an online auction site to give to his wife, who used to work at the Red Barn restaurant on Electric Avenue, Lewistown.

'.. hit the Red Barn.'

Happy Birth DAY!

Fill out card and give to person at counter.

Birth Date

Mo._____ Day _____ Yr. _____

Chief Logan Trading Post: AKA Abie's

By Paul T. Fagley
Burnham

How many of you remember a neighborhood "mom and pop" store near where you grew up? At one time, no matter the town, it seemed there was a store on every other street, and our neighbors owned them. As kids, we all went to the store for penny candy, soda pop, popsicles, and novelty ice creams. Maybe you scoured the neighborhood for pop bottles to take to the store to trade in for a few pennies to buy some candy. When mom was making Sunday dinner, and realized she needed a can of corn, the kids were sent to the store. They were where the local kids hung out. If we were bad, mom and dad knew by the time we got home. How times have changed.

For many who grew up in Burnham, though there were several stores around the town, the one almost all remember was "Abie's." Located behind the YMCA, it was kid central. My family always owned the building, and my parents owned the business in its last years. I believe it was the last neighborhood store in Burnham.

The oldest part of the building was originally located in the Standard Steel parking lot across from Dan's Auto Repair. I believe it may have been a shed originally owned by the Logan Iron and Steel Company, as a part of Emma Furnace, which stood where Bing's Diner is now located. In the mid 1910s, it was a shoe repair shop owned by my great-great-uncle Samuel Wert. According to family stories, around 1918, there was a flood, and it was carried across the intersection to where the Fisher bus garage is now located. He had the building moved to its present location on a property recently purchased by his sister and brother-in-law. Sam continued his business, and also served as tax collector. He died in 1939.

In 1940, Joe Kauffman approached my grandfather to rent the building to

Photo courtesy of Jack Snook

Chief Logan Trading Post

put a store in. The building was small, and the kids called it the "Doghouse," as the Burnham (High School) Bulldog football team hung out there. The school was across the street. Mom said Joe also had a large dog he often had with him in the store. She remembered how he would pet the dog, then hand slice meat without first washing his hands. Within a couple years, Joe sold out to Dyson Kline, and moved across the street and opened a new store in the house. He later decided to build a new store right across the street. Joe never got beyond the foundation, and for many years, the kids hung out on this wall.

Around 1943, Dyson had my grandfather enlarge the building twice to its present size, and added a soda fountain, booths and a jukebox. The kids danced the latest dance craze inside - the Jitterbug, so it became known as the "Jitterbug." With the passing of the dance tax during the war, this soon ended, and Kline turned it into a larger store.

Around 1953, Dyson sold the business to Wayne "Abie" Walker. He first called it "Walker's Trading Post." During the Burnham-Derry-Decatur school mergers, the school across the street be-

came the Chief Logan Junior High School. The students and Abie renamed the business the "Chief Logan Trading Post," and made a sign for the store. When my family took over in 1979, I found this sign in the back of the cellar. Unfortunately, when I tried to retrieve it, it crumbled into dust. After the school became Burnham Elementary, the trading post name was dropped, and the store was officially known as "Walker's Cut-Rate," though both names were used for a time. However, everyone in Burnham called it "Abie's."

In 1979, my parents, Paul J. and Ruth T. Fagley, purchased the business and chose the old name "Chief Logan Trading Post." The store closed in March of 1993, when my parents retired.

Owning and running a neighborhood store meant you were part of the neighborhood. Most of our customers were our neighbors. Many others were patrons from the YMCA, next door. You got to the know the neighborhood kids. They all came to the store.

More times than I could remember, someone would call down to the store and need a few groceries. Often, they were elderly and didn't drive. I would take groceries to their house. Try that with the modern convenience stores we have today! We stocked a good selection of the most common canned and boxed goods. For most of them, we purchased them at the local grocery store and marked them up a few pennies.

We had quite a large candy selection, too. One of our most popular items was the "Swedish red fish." Back in the day, they were sold at a penny a piece, and we counted them one at a time, and put them in a baggie. I often wonder if I counted a million of those fish in the years we owned the store.

In another amusing incident, we noticed that Sour Charms lollipops would sell like hotcakes, and then go dead. A couple months later, they would sell like hotcakes again, and a few weeks later, they would go dead again. We eventually realized it wasn't kids buying them, but women. Pregnant women. We found out that when the Lewistown Hospital had a "Lamaze" childbirth class, these lollipops were used in the method. Seems we were the only store nearby that sold these lollipops. So, the hospital sent the class attendees to our store for them.

Summer evenings were popular for popsicles and novelty ice creams. We had a large selection of these from Hershey's Ice Cream company. Popsicles still sold for a nickel, and later for a dime. Flavors included cherry, grape, orange, lime, vanilla and root beer. Novelties included nutty buddies, orange creamsicles, banjos, fudjos and ice cream sandwiches. We also sold ice cream waffle sandwiches, which we made from the thick boxed slices placed between two waffle biscuits.

When we first took over the store, "soda pop" was still largely sold in returnable glass bottles. We had a "bottle cooler," full of a myriad of flavors. In addition to the standard brands today, there were several local bottlers. Two of them we sold were Wible, based in Saxton, and Snow

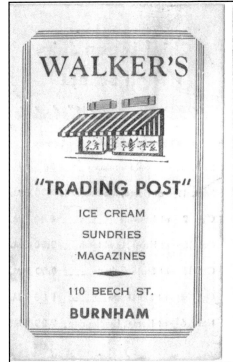

Submitted by Paul Fagley

White, from Three Springs. Later on, during the "Cola Wars," the big boys made deals for shelf space in the large stores that squeezed out the smaller companies. Many of these local bottlers went out of business around this time. The local Royal Crown "RC Cola" distributor was feeling the big store squeeze, and came to us with an offer. For a sizable display space on our floor, we would have a permanent sale price. For years, we sold eight-pack upon eight-pack of RC in 16-ounce glass bottles. I think they started out at 99 cents for an eight-pack. Even then, that was a deal of a price. They once told us we were their biggest seller locally. We were selling so much RC, my parents converted the attached garage into a stockroom.

We sold a lot of soda cold. Two-liter bottles were just becoming a popular size, and we would sell them cold for around $1.29. People started complaining at our price when Jamesway started selling the same bottle for 79 cents. We tried to explain that first, they bought it by the truckload, we didn't. Second, we sold it cold, Jamesway didn't, and third,

we paid $1.20 for that bottle, and sold it cold for a whole 9 cents profit.

During the 1980s and '90s, retailing changed. We could see it. Beginning with the cola wars, stores started competing with each other with the lowest price. Distributors increasingly didn't want to service the smaller independent mom and pop stores. They could sell by the truckload to the chain stores. Gas pumps at the newer convenience stores took more business away. One by one, the neighborhood stores faded into history. We managed to hang on until 1993, when mom and dad decided to retire. We did try to sell the business, though we had some interested people, the banks wouldn't grant loans. We sold off what we could, and auctioned off the rest. Rather than letting the building go vacant, we turned it into a little house. Although we rearranged the windows and doors, we retained the log siding on the front, as a memory of last neighborhood store.

On the internet today, many residents fondly remember the little store as "Abie's." My family was proud to be a part of Burnham's history.

Smith's Gulf, Burnham

Images submitted by Dick Smith, Burnham

A postcard, dated Oct. 16, 1946, circulated in the Burnham area with this image on the front and a message on the back: "Not long ago the corner of Logan Blvd. and Freedom Ave. looked like this ... Perhaps you are wondering about all the activity there now. Soon a new 'Express Stop' Gulf Station, with the last word in Service, will be there to serve you. Watch for the opening date." It was signed: Gulf Oil Corporation.

The postcard was followed by another, dated Nov. 15, 1946. Its message: "Things are shaping up fine. It won't be long before you will be able to get complete service at Gulf's new 'Express Stop' Service Station ... Logan Blvd. and Freedom Avenue. Watch for the opening date.
— Gulf Oil Corporation"

The station opened in 1947, and in 1952, Five years later, Dick and Wiff Smith took it over. The station provided gas, repair and towing service for many years, closing in 2007. A Sheetz convenience store has been built at the site.

Photos submitted by Dick Smith

This aerial photo was taken by Gene Krout in the spring of 1952. Smith's Gulf station is on the left at the intersection, circled. Dick Smith points out that the Burnham Freight Station can be seen at the upper left in the photo.

U.S. Savings stamps were a special
promotion offered by Smith's Gulf.

Submitted by Dick Smith

Smith's Gulf
1965

Smith's Gulf
Final days

Remembering Burnham

Editor's note: This is an abridged version of an article that originally appeared in "I Remember When ... II," a special section published by The Sentinel in 2009.

By Linda Kochenderfer
Burnham

Having been born and raised in Burnham, I have many fond memories of a bygone era — things and places that will never be again. Those were the times that mothers could let their children go out to play with no fear of abduction or any of the other fears we have today. We knew everybody on our streets and probably three or four streets around us.

Money was scarce, but we didn't need a lot of extras. Balls, books and some toys were all we needed.

My life actually started on Freedom Avenue in an apartment over Jim Moore's grocery store. I lived there six years.

We then moved to Seventh Avenue, to a two-story house. But times were tough and my family rented the top floor. We all shared one bathroom and for a couple of years, we all survived.

I really remember the delivery people who traveled to our street. The Purity Milk Company would deliver milk to our house, at first putting it on the porch, then in an insulated box to protect it better. That was when cream was on top of the bottle.

Then there was the meat man. Mr. Baker from Baker's Meat Market on Freedom Avenue made a refrigerated truck to sell his product. I can see him opening the lids and inside were beautiful cuts of meat, lunchmeat and cheese, and sometimes he would give you a slice of cheese. What a treat!

The dry cleaners delivered your clothes to your door, and the Jewel Tea Co. came to sell you coffee and tea items.

These pictures and the one on the next page are reproduced from "Burnham Pennsylvania Historical Book Golden Jubilee 1911-1961," courtesy of the Mifflin County Historical Society.

The Dairy Belle was on Logan Boulevard.

The Burnham Drive-In Theatre was built in 1950.

Ike & Sons Cities Service also was on Logan Boulevard.

One of the most interesting and different peddlers came in a big, yellow school bus, driven by a man we all called Big Al. His name was Al Wildermuth. I guess you could call his bus a "G.C. Murphy on wheels." He came to your door, the ladies stepped in and shopped.

Another well-known peddler was John T. Mitchell. He was known for wonderful corn that he raised.

One of the most wonderful smells on Sixth and Seventh avenues was Beaver Brothers Bakery. Run by the Beaver brothers, it made, without a doubt, the best sticky buns, hard rolls and bread you could ever want. My dad loved fresh bread and every day it was my job to get a loaf of bread. I don't think it always came home square, as I sometimes hung it over my arm and squashed it in the middle.

At the bottom of Seventh Avenue was a mom and pop grocery store run by Mary and Jim Wentle. They also made delicious hoagies. After them, the store was run by George Stoicheff, and later it became the 701 Mart, run by Dave Stoicheff.

Our biggest industry in Burnham was, of course, Standard Steel. In my younger years, it was known as Baldwin Lima Hamilton, then Freedom Forge and Standard Steel. It represented a lot of jobs for Burnham and surrounding areas.

There are many things to remember about them. One is the pounding from the forge shop that vibrated, rattled and moved your items off the shelves.

Nothing could beat the appearance of the sidewalks in Burnham in the '50s. You would open your front door to black sidewalks and everyone's footprints would be there — the men going to work, the kids going to school — everybody left their footprint. This was before the Standard changed fuels. Coal ash was the culprit in this mess. Everybody had to sweep their sidewalks — it was a necessity.

At the bottom of Sixth Avenue was Musser's Bar and Restaurant, spotlessly clean, serving meals to Standard employees and others at lunch time, and ice cream cones to the kids in the evening.

Stewart's Restaurant

We had two grocery stores in Burnham. At the corner of Fifth Avenue was Tony's Clover Leaf Grocery Store, run by Tony Soccio and his wife. The second one was on Fourth Avenue, called Stuckey's IGA, run by the Stuckey family. We didn't have far to go to pick up our everyday groceries.

We also had our own doctor. Dr. James McNabb had his office on the Fourth Avenue corner, across from Stuckey's Store. He treated a lot of the residents of Burnham and the surrounding area.

At the bottom of Beech Street, there was a small convenience store run by Abe Walker. We called it Abby's. He sold penny candy for the kids, ice cream, bread and milk and other sundries. It was later called Chief Logan Trading Post, and run by the Fagley family.

Our funeral home at the time was Speer's Funeral Home, run by Bill Speer. I can vividly remember that he put a fish pond right in front of the steps. You could view your loved ones and see the fish at the same time. It is now Heller Hoenstine Funeral Home.

Burnham Hardware has been there since 1949. It was built by Jim and Helen Kochenderfer as a small hardware, and later, in 1961, the rest was added. They ran it for 25 years and then their son, James, wife and son still run it today.

Around the corner was Sheetz Brothers gas station, run by Ira and Bill Sheetz. It sat at the triangle of Walnut and Elm streets. It was a Sinclair, full service gas station. The building is now

Dan's Auto Repair garage.

There were several small businesses on Freedom Avenue. One that stood out was "Japs" Barber Shop and small convenience store. He offered free advice, haircuts and a place to hang out. Run by Ira Snook, it was "the place" to be on Freedom Avenue.

Near the end of Freedom Avenue, Hambright Brothers Hardware offered a full line of hardware products.

On the corner of South Walnut and Freedom Avenue was a restaurant run by the Oburn family. It was then sold to Mike and Frank Battista. During that time, the building burned, a new building was built and later bought by John Stewart. At the side of the restaurant was a small building where Tom Bigelow ran his barber shop. Both were places where the guys loved to hang out. The building was torn down and is now Bing's Diner.

I can remember going to the Burnham Train Station, which was located by the tracks near the Standard parking lot. The building wasn't big, but the train would stop and they would fill the cart with packages. Inside, there was a pot-belly stove to keep you warm in the winter.

On the other side of the tracks, Gus's Pizza had a shop, and after that, Ruble's opened their donut shop. Klingler Produce is now in that location.

Hoffman Concrete was across the road. They supplied concrete to the area for a long time. C. DeVecchis and Sons bought the business and ran it until closure. Creekside Hearth and Patio is now in that location.

Glace's Filling Station

Glace's Filling Station, shown in these photos from the 1930s, was located at the intersection of Freedom Avenue and Logan Boulevard in Burnham, where most recently, Mattress World was situated. The station was operating during the time when gas stations sold different brands of gas, illustrated by the different gas pumps.

Photos submitted by Walter Glace, Burnham

The smell of fresh bread ...

Sketch history of the Beaver Brothers Bakery

By Paul Fagley
Burnham

For three quarters of a century, Burnham was scented with the smell of fresh bread and pastries baking. Located on the corner of North Beech Street and Sixth Avenue, the former "Econopane" building was a bakery with an interesting history. It was here that a man of mechanical genius built a bakery and machine shop, and brought innovations to the baking industry.

Born in 1867 in Dortmond, Germany, Hugo Gottschalk learned the baking trade before coming to America in 1884. By 1886, he had settled in Reedsville, and worked at local bakeries. He would open his own small bake shops before building the Standard Bakery at the corner of Sixth Avenue and Beech Street in Burnham in 1905. He soon added a machine shop and began developing baking equipment, much of which is still used today. One of his first was the automatic pan cleaning and greasing machine, for which he received a patent in 1908. He followed that with a dough mixer in 1911, and four years later the automatic brick oven for baking, where the bread was sent through the oven on a conveyor. This latter invention he first used at a new bakery he opened in Mifflin, Juniata County.

After only a few years, he sold the bakeries to concentrate on manufacturing his equipment in Burnham, and later at a new machine shop in Reedsville. He also purchased the Reedsville (aka Morrison) Hotel (later known as the Black Horse Tavern) in 1919, and opened another bake shop on the first floor. He continued to operate the hotel and bake shop until his death in 1936.

Hugo's most lasting contribution to

Standard Bakery
Burnham
1910s

Photos courtesy of Mifflin County Historical Society

the area citizens, however, had nothing to do with bakeries or inventions. In 1905, he was instrumental in the establishment of Lewistown Hospital, raising funds to build the hospital by holding horse and pony shows! He donated lands in Reedsville, where he lived, and built a horse track. Today, this parcel of land is the Youth Park. He also purchased artificial daisies in Germany for sale to establish the nurses home next to the hospital. This home, later to become offices, was torn down only a few years ago.

After Hugo sold the bakery, it passed through a succession of owners, including the Rev. Harry Spanogle, who purchased it in 1918. In 1922, Guy, Park, and Ellis Beaver purchased the plant, with another brother, Carl, joining in 1925. The name was changed to the Beaver Brothers Bakery. In that same year, their father, J. O. Beaver, began to

deliver bakery goods to homes in the area. The first delivery vehicle was a horse-drawn wagon, equipped with drawers in which to place the goods. The wagon was pulled using a Belgium horse purchased from a local Amish farmer.

The bakery continued to expand through the years, both in production and in area of distribution. Products were sold from Mount Union to Selinsgrove, from State College to Duncannon. Breads and rolls were later sold under the American Beauty label, which included a red rose on the wrapper. And who could resist those mouth-watering sweet goods the Beavers were noted for. One of their best-selling baked goods was their Old-Fashioned Sticky Buns, a perennial favorite.

In the aftermath of the 1972 Hurricane Agnes flood, the bakery achieved another claim to fame, when

Gottschalk trademark

it donated 5,000 loaves of bread to area flood victims. Just a couple of months later, in December of that year, the Beavers closed the bakery. The closing meant the loss of 125 jobs, and a combined payroll of over $1 million. The steep price increases of flour since the flood a few months earlier was also cited as a reason. For a while, it was a distribution center for Tender Touch bread. No more would the pleasing aroma of baking bread and sweet goods fill the air of Burnham.

For many years, the building was the home of the Econopane Insulating Glass Company.

American Beauty bag

Submitted by
Paul Fagley

Beaver Brothers Bakery
Old-Fashioned Cinnamon Buns
A One-time Bakery Secret Recipe*

*Kindly given to the Burnham community by
Ellis Beaver and family.*

Ingredients – Dough:

10 cups of flour	1/2 cup sugar
1/2 cup shortening	3 cups of water
1 tbsp. salt	1-1/4 oz. yeast
1 egg	

Ingredients – Old-Fashioned Mix:

1-1/2 lbs. sugar	3/4 oz cinnamon
2-3/4 oz water	6 oz shortening

Instructions – Old-Fashioned Mix:

1. Add a little water to the cinnamon and stir.
2. Add sugar and rest of water.
3. Mix and add shortening slowly.

Instructions – Dough:

1. Mix dough ingredients together and roll out to about 1/4-inch thick, in a rectangular shape.
2. Spread old-fashioned mix on entire dough, using all of the mix.
3. Roll tightly and cut into 3/4 inch thick pieces.
4. Lay out on ungreased cookie sheet and bake at 325 degrees until done. (6-8 minutes average)
5. After removing from oven, dump buns into a cold pan for a minute or two and allow the mix to soak into the buns.

Yields: 10-12 buns.   *Recipe scaled down to family size.

"... In 1905, Hugo Gottschalk was instrumental in the establishment of Lewistown Hospital, raising funds to build the hospital by holding horse and pony shows!"

Beaver Brothers Bakery

The Beaver Brothers Bakery, at the corner of North Beech Street and Sixth Avenue, Burnham, is pictured in the 1920s. The picture is courtesy of the Guy Beaver family.

The picture of Beaver's Bread truck in the 1960s is courtesy of the Mifflin County Historical Society, John Gingerich Collection.

Hannon's Store and Restaurant

Hannon's Store and Restaurant, shown here in about 1945, was the first fruit market on Logan Boulevard, Burnham, according to Jim Hannon, who said his father, W.R Hannon, owned the store.

It was located near Standard Steel to serve the people who worked there.

Hannon was the first to sell produce at the Belleville sale on Wednesdays, and also sold produce in Centre County on Tuesdays.

In 1958, Jim's dad had a heart attack, and Jim, who was serving in the U.S. Air Force in Germany, received a hardship discharge to come back home to help with the family business. He said that while he was in Germany, he told a merchant that his bananas were too expensive, and showed him a picture of his father's produce market. An instant bond between the two was formed.

Submitted by Jim Hannon, Burnham

Price's Service Station

Price's Service Station and Restaurant was located on Electric Avenue, on the curve near Kish Park. This interior view, photographed in 1941, shows four men seated at the counter, a waitress serving them, and a cook in the doorway. A large, Juniata Ice Cream sign hangs on a wall, while rows of bells extend from the ceiling.

Photo courtesy of the Mifflin County Historical Society

Standard Steel Works,

Burnham, Pa.

STEEL TIRES

Wrought Iron Centres,
Steel Tired Wheels.

GENERAL OFFICE:

220 S. 4TH STREET,

PHILADELPHIA.

REPRESENTATIVES:

CHICAGO, 1013 Monadnock Bldg.
Fitz-Hugh & Spencer.

ST. LOUIS, 516 North Third St.
Andrew Warren.

Book page courtesy of Pam Goss, Lewistown

Standard Steel

From "Lewistown, Penna. As It Is," published in 1894, courtesy of Pam Goss, of Lewistown

"A leading seat of industry in Mifflin County is at Burnham, three miles north of Lewistown.

"Here the Standard Steel Company have for years been leaders in the manufacture of steel tires for locomotive wheels, their product being of the highest quality and most skillful construction, well meriting the name of 'Standard.'

Within a few years they also manufacture high-grade wheel centres, and have just added a complete open-hearth plant for the manufacture of their own steel.

They have substabtial buildings throughout, mammoth engines and hammers, the latest improved machinery, hydraulic and electrical cranes and a modern electric lightning and power plant, with their own railroad tracks and locomotive."

•••

Since its beginnings in 1795, Standard Steel remains a leading manufacturer of forged steel wheels and axles for freight railcars, locomotives and passenger railcars. The company was No. 3 in the Pennsylvania Department of Labor and Industry's 2016 Top 50 Employers list for Mifflin County.

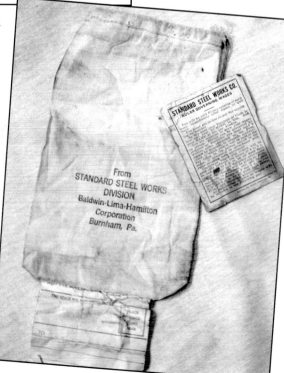

From
STANDARD STEEL WORKS
DIVISION
Baldwin-Lima-Hamilton
Corporation
Burnham, Pa.

A money bag that would have held a Standard Steel Works employee's pay is a piece of memorabilia in the collection of Susan and Carl King, of Lewistown

Merry Christmas - 1942

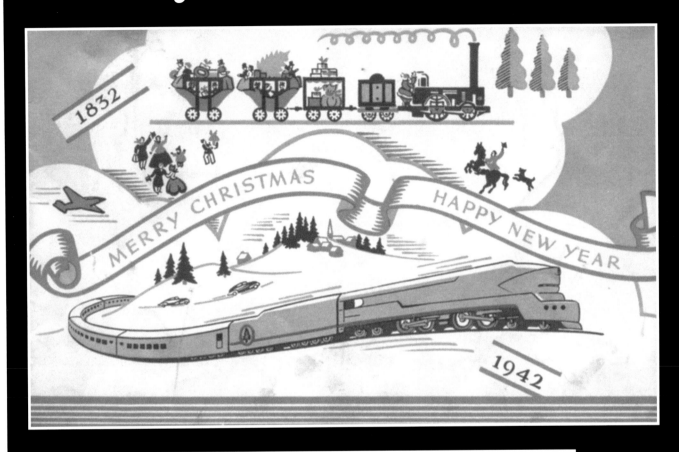

To All Members of the Baldwin Family

Though the whole world is in turmoil and though our Country is at war, nevertheless we may take comfort and satisfaction from the fact that America is not waging a campaign of conquest. Rather we citizens of the United States are devoting our strength, our possessions and our lives, if need be, to the end that mankind may be finally and forever rid of the ruthlessness and cruelty of the dictator; and thus once more free to tread the paths of happiness and peace.

We fight for the right; not selfishly but with the knowledge of great sacrifices yet to be made, cheerfully and willingly for the cause of decency and justice. That once again, in some year not far distant, the Christmas bells may ring out their message, "Peace on Earth, Good Will toward Men."

You have my most sincere good wishes for happiness on this Christmas Day and during the New Year.

President
The Baldwin Locomotive Works

DECEMBER 25, 1942

From the collection of Sondra Griffith, of Yeagertown

Standard Steel, in Burnham, was once a division of Baldwin Locomotive Works.

Busy as a Fisher Honey Bee

By Sarah Fisher Hill
Granville

My father, Merle P. Fisher, developed such a craving for honey as a teenager that it occurred to him that there would be a simple remedy. A few bees would cost little and would supply him with all the honey he could eat. Merle secured his first hive of bees in 1938. It all started as a hobby, with that one hive. Eight years later, he became a full-time beekeeper, with 75 hives.

By 1960, he had grown to more than 1,500 hives.

Merle's business was located on the family farm in Granville, Mifflin County. The farm is along the Juniata River. Merle's beekeeping was a busy life. When the honey flow locally had fallen off, he sought the advice of E.J. Anderson, professor of beekeeping at Penn State. Professor Anderson explained that hard work is not enough for successful beekeeping. Weather conditions must be considered, and, in addition, the bees must be taken to localities where flowers furnish the best flow of honey.

That set my father on a series of journies, covering hundreds of miles. He trucked his bees from place to place, wherever the promise of honey flow was the richest. Moves were made just after darkness, when the bees are most docile and in the hive for the night. Usually the entrances were screened into their hives for travel. Upon arrival at their new location, the screens were removed, using a little smoke to soothe the bees during unloading.

The season opened with pollination work among orchards in Franklin and Adams counties in Pennsylvania. The orchard growers would pay for the bees to be placed on their properties. It then moved to clover in Snyder County in Pennsylvania, and to Washington County in Maryland. The buckwheat honey flow was in the

Photo submitted by Sarah Fisher Hill
Beekeeper Merle P. Fisher

northeastern section of Pennsylvania. The last crop, before cold weather set in, was goldenrod and aster.

In the fall, after the honey crop was removed, the bees were prepared to be taken to Florida for the winter. There, the hives were placed in orange groves. Merle started this so it was possible to harvest the entire fall honey crop. Then, in spring, the bees supplied a crop of orange blossom honey.

For many winters, the Fisher family would live in Clearwater, Florida, in the days when Clearwater was just dirt roads. The school-age children would go to school in Florida for three months. Then, when it was time for orchard pollination, the family would return to Pennsylvania. In the 1950s and '60s, he was the largest migratory beekeeper in the eastern part of the United States.

On the farm, my father had a honey house where the supers of honey would be extracted and packed. Merle jarred his honey in eight-ounce, one-pound, two-pound and five-pound sizes. He sold his honey to local markets, as well as to wholesale packing companies, in 60-pound cans, and 55-gallon drums. The process in the honey house was a family affair. Merle and his wife, Emily (Vogt), had 10 children, so all helped at various times.

When there was new comb to be put in the frames, it was often the older children's job. As Merle worked the bee yards in the summer, the new comb was put on the hives where needed.

Merle was very involved in the Pennsylvania State Beekeepers Association, serving as president many times over the years. He also lectured

Photos submitted by Sarah Fisher Hill

Merle Fisher, left, attends the Pennsylvania Farm Show.

to classes at Penn State University earlier in his beekeeping career. He was instrumental in starting the Pennsylvania State Honey Queen program. Pennsylvania had several queens go on to be American Honey Queen.

The Girl Scout camp was located along the Juniata River, and as camps were held there in the summer, one mile from the Fisher farm, a regular walking field trip was going to the Honey House. There they were shown the process of extracting the honey from the combs, and each girl received a two-ounce jar of honey.

Earlier in his career, Merle sold Italian queen bees that he raised, which were shipped all over the United States. He served as a mentor to many young beekeepers. His second son, Dyson, became a commercial beekeeper as well.

Merle participated in the Pennsylvania Farm Show, starting in 1932. He did many, many large individual entries, as well as different varieties of honey. He won many prizes for his honey, comb honey and wax entries. Merle also manned the booth of the State Beekeepers Association, where they sold honey and honey-sweetened ice cream. Later, he managed the booths at the Farm Show and the Ag Progress fair for more

Merle, right, and his son, Dyson, work in the field. Below, Merle wears a bee veil.

Emily Vogt Fisher
(Merle's wife), with
rolling pin, bakes
using honey in her
recipes, with some
of the Fisher chil-
dren, from left,
Sarah (Sally), Lu-
cinda, Timothy,
Mary and Ruth.
Photo taken in 1960.

Photos submitted by
Sarah Fisher Hill

than 25 years.

Merle was a quiet man, but he loved to talk about bees and the importance of the work the little insect does for agriculture. He was ready to answer others' questions and to mentor young beekeepers.

Merle hauled his last load of bees to apple orchards at the age of 86. He always remarked that we should work as long as possible. Merle died at the age of 92. He was one of the best known bee-keepers on the east coast, and a member of the state association from 1941 until his death. In 1980, he achieved the honor of being named Beekeeper of the Year from the state association.

Merle Fisher
2005

Today, his grandsons, the sons of the late W. Dyson Fisher, carry on the love of beekeeping under their own name. Their bee business is one of the largest in the United States. My dad was especially proud that his love of bees is being carried on in the family.

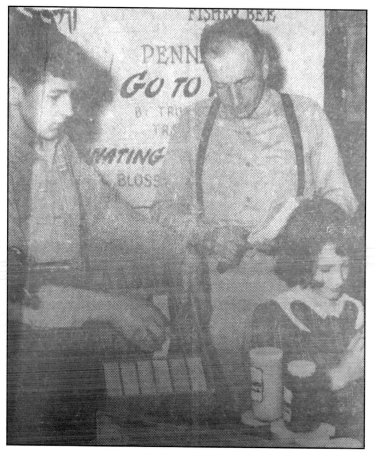

Merle Fisher, in center, with son, Dyson, and daughter, Lois, set up a Farm Show exhibit in 1960.

Market St., McVeytown, PA

Photo submitted by Carrol "Sis" Norton

Norton's Pro Hardware, McVeytown

Norton's Pro Hardware

McVeytown: 1968-1992

By Carrol "Sis" Norton
McVeytown

It was early summer in 1968. One Saturday morning, Jim returned to our apartment in McVeytown and asked me what my thoughts were in regard to us buying a hardware store. I thought I was hearing things, but asked, "Whose hardware store?"

He said, "I just came from spending some time with Bill Baker and he has his store for sale and I thought we should consider buying it."

A few years before, Bill had bought Novak's Store that sat on the corner where the Kish Bank is now located, and after a year or so he bought the Florence Witherow property on Market Street, remodeled it and moved his store to that location.

Jim was still employed at New Holland in Belleville. He said, "I could work out a notice and we could take the plunge and go into the hardware business."

So, he and Bill, along with Zelda, worked on the inventory so we could get an idea about how much money we would need to borrow. That went on for a few weeks and finally we arrived at a figure, so we then decided to check out a lending institution.

I had worked at the McVeytown Branch of the First National Bank of Lewistown for 13 years and thought we would start there for a loan. We couldn't believe it when we were turned down because we drove nice looking automobiles, and something looking automobiles, and something

about our lifestyle, and we would probably not be able to have a successful business.

Bummer, we thought, so plan number two went in to effect. We then went to see Dave Brown at the Russell National Bank in Lewistown. That was a Friday evening and we got a call the next Tuesday informing us we should come in and sign papers for the loan.

That scared us half to death, as it sounded so easy.

It all worked out and we got the loan. One day I was working at the McVeytown Post Office and one of the employees mentioned about the sale of the hardware store and was wondering who might be buying it. I never said a word.

Photo submitted by Carrol "Sis" Norton

Jim and Sis Norton set up a display at the Rothrock Fair for their store.

Jim worked out his notice and left New Holland. We took over the business in June of 1968 and the new adventure began at Norton's Hardware.

We got to know wonderful people, and I remember many of the old timers like Mooch and Mary South, Noah Fagan, Peck Kirk, Don Kerr, my uncles, Hyde and Mack Rodkey and many more coming into the store to get their fishing and hunting license. You had to fill out a form, and many of them would ask Jim or me to fill it out for them. I guess they thought it would take them too long to fill in the blanks. They would sign the form for us and they were then on their way.

Many times Mary Wooding would bring us something from her attic for

Jim to repair, and Ruth Swigart one day brought her electric iron and wanted to know if Jim could put a new cord on it. Muriel Hanawalt came down through our back yard with her reel mower and asked Jim to sharpen it for her. Merrill Wray had a cutting blade for on his tractor and Jim kept it sharpened for him. He also did things for Hazel Price, and Velva Rodgers was a regular customer, along with many more wonderful folks from the McVeytown area. Then there were those who needed windows repaired, new screen put in their storm door inserts, guys who would bring their chainsaws in for Jim to sharpen, and I could go on and on.

In 1972, when we were building our house, Jim was helping with that

project and I was at the store, so I learned to do many of these things and was pretty good at applying the glaze to windows, if I must say so myself.

My sister, Marj Davidson, would come from New Jersey in the winter with Bobby, Billy and Beth, and Beth would come in the summer. They loved being at the hardware store. Marj often wonders how in the world Jim put up with three kids for biggest part of a day at the hardware store. If they got unruly, Jim would put them at various spots in the store and would give them something to do. Sometimes I think it was pounding nails in a board.

Beth was only 4 or 5 years old at the time, and she loved sitting on the

Photos submitted by Carrol "Sis" Norton

**Memorabilia from
Norton's Pro Hardware**

little ladder behind the cash register. She thought it was wonderful when she could turn the crank on the cash register and the drawer flew open. She even learned how to make change.

My Uncle Hyde Rodkey always checked in to the store after lunch and spent an hour or so with Jim or whoever was on duty, and we looked forward to that every day.

We loved when Virgie Youtzy came down from the upstairs apartment and visited with us, and quite often Clarence Scheffel stopped in to see what was going on. And then there was John Koch, who always timed it right as he knew what time I left the post office to go to the store for lunch, and many times John had lunch with us.

We always looked forward to our salesmen arriving, and they were great men to work with and kept the store well stocked with lots of items.

Sometimes on a Sunday we would get a call that someone needed something from the store and, living on Market Street at the time, we would accommodate that person to help them take care of their problem.

Jim was a handy man and if he didn't have the part to repair an item, he would make it. It is hard to find guys like that today.

When Country Memories Day started we always found our spot in front of our store and loved being a part of that big day. Then, in September, it was the Rothrock Fair, and we loved participating in that event with our stand displaying many hardware items.

When the fire siren went off, Jim was out the door, ran to the fire-

house, fired up the fire truck and in no time he was pulling out with the junior firemen on the truck. That was when my mom arrived at the store and kept shop until I got done working at the post office, or when Jim returned from a fire, accident or whatever.

There were times when a customer would come in and ask Jim if he had a certain item, saying he looked all over Lewistown for it, and to think he could have gotten it right here in McVeytown at Norton's Hardware.

We started out as Norton's Hardware and in later years became known as Norton's Pro Hardware, an update regarding dealing with C. H. Miller in Huntingdon, Pa.

Mom, Helen Moist, was our major helper and she loved being at the store. Charlie Rowe was build-

ing his home in Bratton Township, and he would send his wife, Ninevah, to the store for supplies. He would always tell her to not talk long with Helen, as he needed to get his job done. They were lovely people to deal with.

Mom and I ran the store when we were building the White House on the Hill as Jim worked right along with the guys from Jack Hess Inc., and then, after the exterior was completed, Jim was on his own and finished the entire inside of the house, which was completed December of 1972.

Mom and I continued to keep shop until our house was finished, then she decided it was time to retire, so we hired Dorothy Pollock and Miriam Kimberly. They learned the ropes of the hardware business, and it was wonderful having them on board for several years. When they decided to give it up, we hired Mary Miller Reed. It was great having Mary working for us, and she stayed with us until we sold the business in June of 1992.

Looking back now sort of chokes one up, as so many of our patrons are no longer with us, but we have wonderful memories of all those who graced the door of our store and would do it again in a heartbeat.

A big thank you to the then Russell National Bank, now the First National Bank of Pennsylvania, who almost 50 years ago had the confidence in us to give us the money to take on such an adventure, and the residents of McVeytown and surrounding areas were good to us. It was a wonderful 24 years in the hardware business.

God is good!

Jos. Strode's Store

The back of this 1880s advertising card, below, indicates that it is from the Joseph Strode Dry Goods Store in Strode's Mills, as it was spelled in that era. The card was scented with Hoyt's German cologne, which was sold at the store. Strode's store offered dry goods, groceries, drugs, medicines, shoes, hardware, crockery, etc. The card is from the collection of Chris Kearns, of Lewistown.

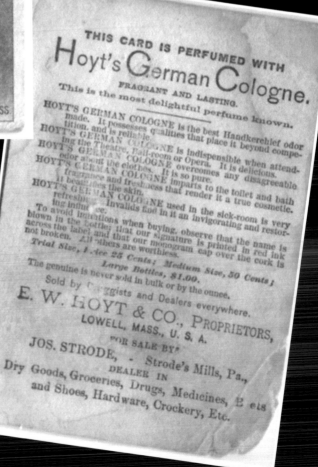

Music man

Stade's Music Store Lewistown

By Freda Stade Richard
Lewistown

1936, the year of the flood, my birth, and the year Karl Stade moved his business of "importer of fine musical merchandise" from 4 N. Main St. in Yeagertown, to 146 Valley Street in Lewistown.

He bought the Valley Street property and turned half into a store with its own entrance and display window, and the other half into a studio for private lessons. The family lived behind and above the store. Even though the store kept regular 9 to 5 hours, closed Wednesday afternoons, open until 9 on Saturdays, customers could get emergency supplies by ringing the doorbell.

Family members "worked" in the store as their abilities and schedules permitted. I personally don't remember ever getting a stipend, but if I needed 15 cents to go to a movie matinee, I knew where to find it. Mother had the wash hung up, or the dough rising before the store opened at 9, and she would be needed to wait on customers.

During the '40s and '50s there were three music stores in Lewistown, each one specializing in a different aspect of the music business. Most of the local band directors and piano teachers ordered their music through Stade's Music Store. In addition, all instrument repairs were completed in house. The store sold pianos, sheet music, band and orchestra instruments, guitars, twirling batons, harmonicas, drum sticks, reeds, strings, picks and kazoos. In addition, Mr. Stade had a Fuller Brush franchise and sold Emerson radios.

Mr. Stade had his formal musical training at the Hamel Conservatory of Music in Germany. After a circuitous path through the vaudeville

Submitted by Freda Stade Richard

105

houses and silent movie theaters of Brooklyn, New York and Williamsport, he came to Mifflin County to teach in the Derry Township School District. During his tenure there, his students and orchestras received top awards in music competitions around the state. In 1950, he conducted the TWUA Symphony Orchestra, the Grace Evangelical Church orchestra, and performed as cello soloist for area events.

Mr. Stade died in 1958. The Valley Street property was sold. His wife, Louise, survived him by 35 years.

Freda Stade stands in front of Stade's Music Store, 146 Valley Street, Lewistown, in 1952.

Photos submitted by Freda Stade Richard

Yeagertown

A 1932 receipt from the Yeagertown Garage, with service stations owned by W.B. Wagner at 135 Logan St., Lewistown, and Main Street in Yeagertown, is from the collection of Susan and Carl King, of Lewistown.

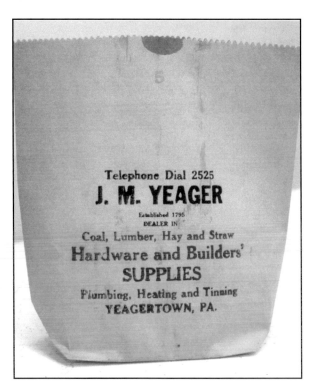

A bag from the J. M. Yeager Hardware and Builders' Supplies company, Yeagertown, is from the collection of Gene Hughes, of Lewistown.

Riden's Restaurant

From and article originally published in The Sentinel on Oct. 10, 2003:

Riden's Restaurant in Yeagertown was established in 1917 as Naum Stoichess Public Restaurant and Grocery, owned by Naum and Ristina Stoichess, who came to America from Macedonia. The picture above was taken in the 1920s or early '30s. The picture below shows an interior view in the restaurant's early years. Three generations of the Riden-Stoichess family served customers from the corner of Derry and North Derry avenues in Yeagertown before the restaurant closed. The Stoichess family lived above the restaurant, including four children, Cecilia (Ceil), Ann, Luba and Stanley. Luba eventually went on to open her own restaurant in Burnham, named Luba's. In 1947, Ceil married Jack Riden, and they eventually inherited the business, which they ran for more than 60 years, with help from their children.

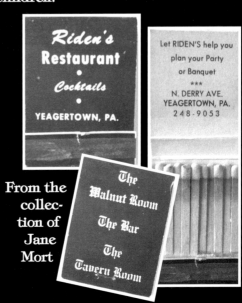

From the collection of Jane Mort

Riden's Restaurant
• Cocktails •
YEAGERTOWN, PA.

Let RIDEN'S help you plan your Party or Banquet
***
N. DERRY AVE. YEAGERTOWN, PA.
248-9053

The Walnut Room
The Bar
The Tavern Room

Charles Schaaf Complete Food Market

Michael Aumiller, of Reedsville, submitted a photo of the original flyer for the Charles Schaaf Complete Food Market, which opened June 7, 1951, in Reedsville. The gentleman in the picture above is Charles Schaaf, and the lady is his wife, Vera. See more photos on the next page.

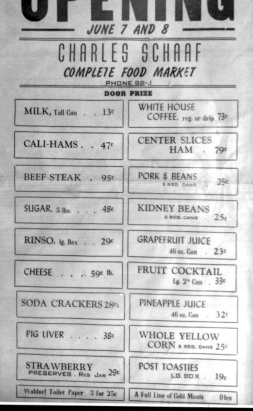

ANNOUNCING

OPENING

JUNE 7 AND 8

CHARLES SCHAAF
COMPLETE FOOD MARKET
PHONE 98-J

DOOR PRIZE

MILK, Tall Can . . 13¢	WHITE HOUSE COFFEE, reg. or drip 73¢
CALI-HAMS . . 47¢	CENTER SLICES HAM . 79¢
BEEF STEAK . 95¢	PORK & BEANS 3 REG. CANS 25¢
SUGAR, 5 lbs. . . . 48¢	KIDNEY BEANS 3 REG. CANS . 25¢
RINSO, lg. Box . . 29¢	GRAPEFRUIT JUICE 46 oz. Can . 23¢
CHEESE . . . 59¢ lb.	FRUIT COCKTAIL lg. 2½ Can . 33¢
SODA CRACKERS 28¢	PINEAPPLE JUICE 46 oz. Can . 32¢
PIG LIVER . . . . 38¢	WHOLE YELLOW CORN 2 REG. CANS 25¢
STRAWBERRY PRESERVES . Reg Jar 29¢	POST TOASTIES LG. BOX . 19¢
Waldorf Toilet Paper 3 for 25¢	A Full Line of Cold Meats Oleo

Charles Schaaf and his food market in Reedsville.

Photos submitted by Michael Aumiller

Doc Sankey's

Serving the Reedsville area for 60+ years

Contributed and compiled by Sankey grandchildren and cousins:

Patricia Ramsey-Macomber, Fairport, New York

Nancy Robson, Port Royal, Pennsylvania

Michelle Ramsey-Hansen, Lancaster, New York

Ella Gahagan, Reedsville, Pennsylvania

John Sankey, Harvey's Lake, Pennsylvania

For more than 60 years Sankey's Drug Store was one of the main businesses in Reedsville.

The owner and proprietor was Foster J. Sankey, who was known in the community as "Doc Sankey." He was known by that title because Doc would treat family and customers with his private label medicine mixes and tinctures, offer advice or administer a bit of first aid after some mishap or bar fight at the Black Horse across the street.

One of his granddaughters remembers it as a "great place to visit and explore," but only as an adult realized its importance to the community.

Foster Sankey graduated from the Philadelphia College of Pharmacy in 1910. In that era, it was required that "at least two years of practical experience in Retail Drug and Apothecary Business" be completed before an individual could own their own "Retail Drug & Prescription Store." Sankey completed that requirement in Philadelphia and then returned to his hometown of Mifflin County.

It was 1916 when he opened his first drugstore at the corner of Main and Logan streets in Reedsville (where the Reedsville National Bank and then Russell National Bank stood).

In 1928, he purchased the property

Photo submitted by Ella Gahagan

Sankey's Drug Store in Reedsville

of the Peter Wertz ice cream and barbershop on the opposite corner and relocated both his business and home there for the next 50 years.

When Sankey bought the building on southwest corner of Main and South Logan streets, there were a lot of renovations that needed to be completed before it was ready for both the household and the drugstore business.

The cellar was dug out to allow for plumbing and heating to be introduced, and the electric system was updated beyond the few lights that were already there.

At the front of the building, where the main store was housed, the ceiling was removed and only a narrow walkway, known as the balcony, remained on the perimeter, suspended some 20 feet above the floor.

In the front of the store, tall plate

glass windows were topped by the Rexall Drug signs. Below the windows, two sidewalk level tin sheet signage proudly displayed the "Sankey's Drug Store" name.

The balcony became the storage area for many boxes, bottles, placards and other items that had or might be needed for display in the front windows. The balcony also became the viewing gallery for the grandchildren during their visits. Either surreptitiously, or by invitation, the door between the store and the dining room upstairs would be opened and the curious eyes and ears of the youngsters would take in a small slice of Reedsville life.

"Be very quiet" the older cousins would remand their younger charges, and a reward of candy promised would help ensure obedience during

Photos submitted by Ella Gahagan, above, and
Patricia Ramsey-Macomber, below

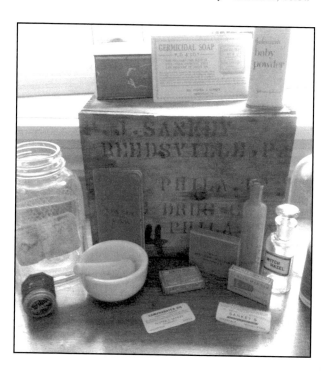

babysitting duty. One of the younger cousins was sure the "candy" was really some of Grandpa's "medicine."

Doc Sankey had what he described as an "old style drug store" and proudly labeled himself as a "druggist."

Labels from bottles in the early years included: Sweet Oil (for a laxative), Lime Water (for stomach acid), and Spirits of Turpentine (for skin irritations). He filled prescriptions of all types, but was best known for his many tonics and medicines based on his self-developed pharmacological mixtures.

His granddaughter, Michelle, remembers with great fondness watching as her grandfather used the flasks, scales, mortar and pestle to compound medications from his own handwritten formulas.

His grandson, John, watched him many hours as well, thinking that his grandfather seemed like a "mad scientist" and marveled that he kept it all straight, never confusing the ingredients of his pharmaceutical recipes or whether the medication being compounded was intended for human or animal treatment.

Medication for the town, farming community and Amish were formulated and mixed in the "back room," an area of the store where only a privileged few were allowed.

During his professional career Mr. Sankey was awarded 15

patents for medications he developed, and patents for seven medications used for veterinary practice.

A granddaughter, Nancy, remembers that his own migraine headaches led her grandfather to formulate what he called his "sick headache" medicine. That mixture's recipe, she later discovered, included high doses of caffeine, and Doc Sankey's own "neutralizing cordial," which helped settle any stomach upset that occurred with that malady. Customers and other family members swore by it for migraine headache relief and would request it by name when they were in need.

Sankey's sunburn medication for application to affected skin and "toothache medicine" (with 0.1 percent methadone) were also popular customer requests.

Ella, another of the granddaughters, loved when she was treated for a bad cold with Sankey's private label cough syrup, as she would lick the bottle edge for a taste of the black licorice flavor, while her cousin remembers dreading the awful taste of that same treatment.

Throughout all the years in business, the drugstore was affiliated with the Rexall brand. Drugs and brand name products being delivered for sale in the store were often delivered by rail to Lewistown, where the packed boxes would be thrown from a slow moving train, recalls his daughter, Peg Sherlock.

The store itself was a cornucopia. Every shelf, counter and display case was crammed with items. Almost always on display were school notebooks, pencil boxes, greeting cards and stationary; gloves, soaps, shampoos, hair coloring products and hair nets; fishing tackle, hooks and sinkers; feminine hygiene products (kept discreetly under the countertop); baby products such as nipples, bottles, formula and pacifiers; shoe polish and shoelaces; combs and brushes; razors, shaving cream and mustache wax; enema bags and foot soaks; nail polish, lipstick and other make-up products; aspirin, milk of magnesia, vitamins Vicks Cough Syrup and sim-

ilar over the counter medicated products; ammunition for shotguns and handguns; licenses for hunting or fishing; seasonal items like Valentine, Christmas or Halloween cards and decorations.

Sparklers were always available for Independence Day celebrations. His oldest grandson, Dick, found a whole cache of fireworks to celebrate Fourth of July in style at home in Juniata County one year as a reward for helping to clear out some of the storeroom areas of the store.

Seasonal candy, chocolates like Whitman boxed candies, and breath mints in tins could be found. Cigarettes, tobacco, and other smoking accoutrements including a box of corncob pipes that sat on the steps leading to the balcony and house above were available for sale. Of course, all the supplies that one might need for taking medication or first aid treatment; measuring spoons, eye drops, band aids and slings, gauze and tape could also be found on those shelves.

All purchases were rung up on the old fashioned cash register located behind the soda fountain. The soda fountain served old fashioned ice cream sodas, cones and milkshakes, as well as Coca Cola made by mixing carbonated water and syrup.

The best part of Sankey's Drug Store, though, had to be the bountiful penny candy case. It was a popular spot in the store and a great place to view all the treats that could be purchased for just a few cents! Wax milk bottles filled with sugar water, spearmint licorice sticks, malted milk balls, Swedish fish, candy cigarettes, gum balls, Tootsie Rolls, Mexican hats, and candy dots on paper, sugar babies, string licorice, jawbreakers and gummy coins. All of his grandchildren anticipated Saturday night during any visits when either an ice cream cone or a bagful of selected candy items could be chosen for only pennies. Not always an easy decision.

Sankey's Drug Store was open some portion of every day of the week and evenings as well. Doc said he worked 14 hour days many years.

Due to Pennsylvania's blue laws, he was closed during the day on Sunday, but opened in the evening for business.

While Prohibition (1920 to 933) was law, it was not uncommon for prescriptions to be filled following instructions like "1 ounce of whiskey at bedtime," and similar directions for using alcohol as medication.

During the depression, he and his wife would serve a cooked noonday meal at the tables and chairs positioned in the middle of the store. The reasonably priced meal helped with income during those tough economic times. Doc once remarked that during the depression there was often a barter system that went on between him and his customers to cover the cost of purchases at the store. Even years later, some customers ran an account for later payment.

All of his daughters had to help out in the store while they were growing up. His daughter, Kathryn Gahagan, continued to be one of his store helpers even after her marriage. Doc's wife, Katherine, spent many hours behind the counter as well. Over the years, various women from town would also work and wait on customers while Doc was busy filling prescriptions and making medications. They also minded the store while he had a mid-day dinner and a half hour nap upstairs.

He always took a week-long vacation when his family was young. Those vacations were extended a bit after the children had left home, but Doc was never away too long. In his later years, Sankey would take off for a half day every Wednesday, and refine his fishing skills. The store's evening hours also became less late as he got up into his 70s and 80s.

Doc said once, when asked, that he still enjoyed running the drugstore well enough and he did not know what he would do if he would retire. He was still working at the age of 89. It wasn't until his death in March 1978, that Sankey's Drug Store and the unique business that it was closed for good. It was the end of an era in Reedsville.

Off the Clipboard

Wed MARCH 15, 1978

By Jim Canfield

Death took one of Reedsville's most respected and beloved residents last week with the passing of Dr. Foster J. Sankey.

Although he led a full life in his 89 years, "Doc" will be sorely missed by a whole parcel of customers from a widespread area who depended on one or more of his secret concoctions to alleviate the pain and discomfort of such ailments as colds, the grippe and rheumatism.

You might say that Doc Sankey was the last of a breed, the very last of the old-time pharmacists who prescribed and made their own preparations. He could count 56 of those preparations that you couldn't buy anywhere else in the world but at "Doc Sankey's in Reedsville."

"Most of my medicines I've had since I started the business," he told this writer during an interview in 1975. "Most I originated myself and some came from my predecessors."

Although the Sankey drugstore had been a mainstay in Reedsville's business life since 1916, the store was actually much older than that, having been founded in 1890. There had been several prior owners before he came on the scene.

A 1907 graduate of the old Lewistown High school on Wayne street, Doc got his degree in pharmaceutical chemistry at the Philadelphia School of Pharmacy and Science. He then worked as a registered pharmacist in Philadelphia for six years while he saved his money so that he could buy his own drugstore. He was influenced to settle in Reedsville by the late Dr. B. R. Kohler.

He made his own medicines in a small laboratory behind the storeroom, and in addition to preparations for humans, he also made them for animals, especially horses, cattle and canines.

His medicines for animals gave him something of an exclusive dealership, or monopoly, in the central part of the state because none of the big drugstores carried them.

Doc Sankey worked long and hard to build up his successful drugstore, even after he fell victim to a heart attack in October of 1974, and a feature story I did on him some years ago concluded with his own personal "preparation" for the long success of his drugstore:

"Work, hard work," he said. "I work hard. The business didn't just grow by itself. It had to have somebody working at it and pushing it."

Clipping submitted by Ella Gahagan

A tribute to Foster Sankey was featured in Jim Canfield's "Off the Clipboard" column in The Sentinel on March 15, 1978.

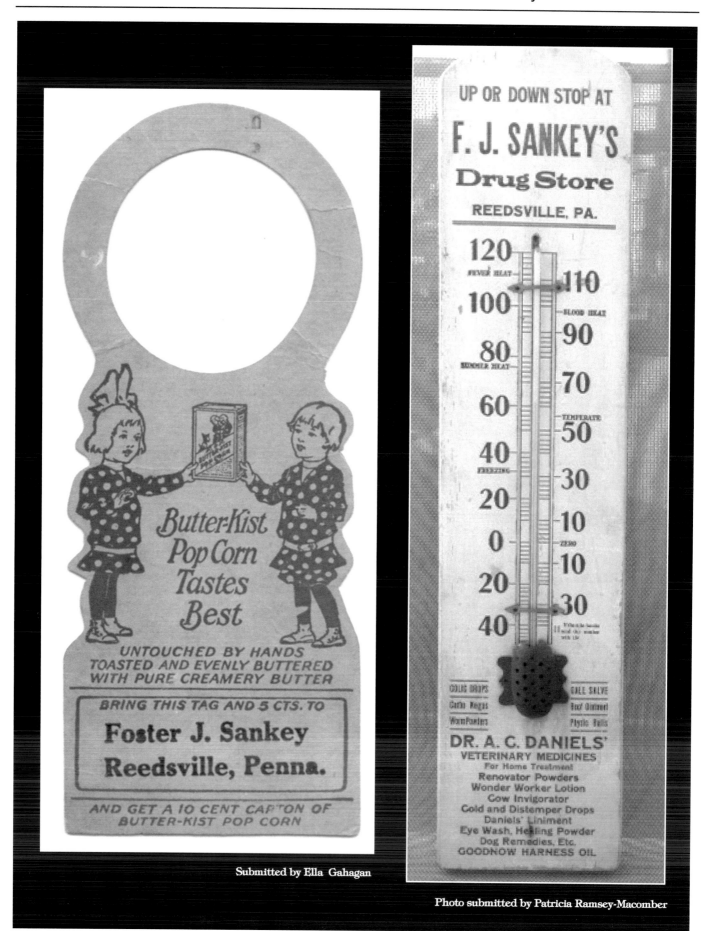

Submitted by Ella Gahagan

Photo submitted by Patricia Ramsey-Macomber

Foster Sankey

A servant to the community

This article was originally published in the Valley Observer newspaper in March 1978:

EDITOR'S NOTE: In March of 1976 we ran a front page feature of Foster J. Sankey concerning the 60th anniversary of being in business in Reedsville. This week we would like to reprint portions of that story in honor of Mr. Sankey, who passed away last week.

"Doc" Sankey 1976

When Foster Sankey opened the doors of his drugstore in Reedsville for the first time it was a presidential election year. To give you an idea of just how long ago that was, the president was Woodrow Wilson and his campaign slogan was, "He kept us out of war."

The year was 1916; the date was March 23, and Foster J. Sankey was 27 years old when he set up shop along Main Street in Reedsville at the site where the Reedsville branch of the Russell Bank now stands.

Most people in Reedsville cannot remember a time when Sankey's wasn't open to serve the residents with their pharmaceutical needs. In 1916, when he opened for business, he was six years older than Babe Ruth, who was then a promising pitcher with the Boston Red Sox.

In March, 1976, "Doc" Sankey talked about his 60 years in business. "I had to work since I was 12," he said. "We were poor; my mother was a widow. I worked in a grocery store while I went to school in Lewistown. The store was where McCrory's now stands."

Foster Sankey was born in Belleville, the son of a butcher, and the family eventually moved to Lewistown after stops in Jefferson County and Yeagertown. Foster was graduated from Lewistown High School with the class of 1907. His burning desire was to be a doctor.

However, then as now, medical school took money, and although he has saved the munificent sum of $35 after work every single day since the age of 12, it still wasn't enough. Medical school was out of the question. By borrowing $200 from his grandfather Sankey, a Belleville potato farmer, he was able to enter the Philadelphia College of Pharmacy, from which he was graduated in 1910.

Although lack of money thwarted his medical career plans, he said, "With what was available, I did the best I could."

After opening his pharmacy in 1916, he stayed at the same location on Main Street until 1928, when the Reedsville National Bank purchased the building as the site for their new offices. Foster moved across the street to that corner. The building was old even then.

"The back part of the building is 150 years old," he said. "They tell me it was once used as a tavern." The front part is approximately a century old. The brick they used came from clay found in Honey Creek.

When Foster moved into his new business location, it was occupied by a barber shop run by Elmer Dippery, and an ice cream parlor run by Peter Wertz. The soda fountain is still there.

During his lifetime, Sankey had seen many changes; not all of the changes were for the better, according to Foster. He had always had a lively trade with the Amish families of the Milroy and Reedsville areas. In recent years, however, Doc found it increasingly more difficult to stock many of the items desired by the Amish. "Many recipes favored by the Amish are not made by the big drug houses any more," he said. Prices jumped drastically on still other items.

Sankey, despite these problems, continued to do the best he could.

When Doc Sankey talked to us in March of our bicentennial year, he commented, "I just want to serve the people for as long as I'm able. The worst thing I can imagine is not to have anything to do."

Photo submitted by Kay Semler

Mifflin County Airport

Keeping passion for flying alive

By Kay Semler
Reedsville

Soon after World War II, Major Harvey J. Hostetler of Belleville, and Capt. William F. Sager Jr., of Lewistown, both former members of the Army Air Forces, conceived the idea for a local airport to keep their passion for flying alive and recognizing that air transportation was the wave of the future.

For Harvey, the excitement for aviation began when he was a student at the Union Mill School, in Belleville, when Sam Burke flew over the school he jumped out the window to see the airplane. This is a story that was told by his sister who was in the same one-room school.

Mifflin County Airport Flight instructors in 1946, in front of a Piper PA-12 aircraft, are, from left, William Sager, Harvey Hostetler, Bill Wilson and Harry Wolfe. Wilson lives in Reedsville and contributed information for this story.

Three airplanes on the left, numbered 1, 2 and 3, were the planes use for flight instruction.

Photo submitted by
Kay Semler

A 147-acre farm was purchased from Parks Murtiff for $16,000, with a red brick house, barn and out-buildings. Harvey and his family lived in the house, which is now the OIP Milroy. Trees were cleared and dips in the terrain were leveled for the 4,000- foot dirt, gravel and grass runway for an August 15, 1946 opening. They made use of the existing buildings for operation while the hangar was built.

As quoted in The Sentinel, "Given a Class 2 rating, there is nothing nearer here to compare with the new enterprise than similarly classified ports in Martinsburg and Williamsport."

Flight instruction under the G.I. Bill of Rights was the main service of the business. Charter service, aircraft and engine repair and sales, and storage of airplanes were provided. Both Sager and Hostetler were instructors for the Army Air Corps, and were joined by Bill Wilson and Harry Wolfe as instructors at Mifflin County, and piloted charter flights.

Two of the airplane inventory were government surplus, and the balance of planes were private purchases by the corporation.

Incorporation papers dated November 18, 1946, were issued by the Commonwealth of Pennsylvania to Mifflin County Air Transport Inc. for the purpose of the transportation

for persons and property by means of aircraft as a common carrier in Pennsylvania, located in R.F.D, Reedsville, Armagh Township, Mifflin County for a term of 50 years.

Eleven shareholders contributed financial support for the project. They included A. Reed Hayes Jr., Harvey J. Hostetler, Charles R. Zook, J.D. Kennedy, John T. Rogers Jr., M.H. Simmons, D.H. Miller, Samuel W. Taylor, H. R. Manbeck, Paul E. Fetterolf, William F. Sager Jr. and G. Clifford Rice.

Bill Wilson recounted that smudge pots were used for runway lights. There was no beacon, expect for a neon sign on the Bel-View Inn that was in direct line of the runway. The runway was never paved, and remained a grass strip.

After several years flight instruction under the G.I. Bill ended, and work for the instructors was reduced, so they moved on to other jobs. Charter service, repairs and fuel sales continued.

Harvey took a job as pilot for two governors of Pennsylvania and the Air Force Reserve. Bill Sager left the area.

To augment income at the airport, tomatoes and peas were grown along the runways and sold to Mifflin County Packing Company, owned by A. Reed Hayes and Roland Thompson. A large farmer's market and

auctions were held at the airport.

Eugene Kraut became the manager of the airport, followed by Lanny McCoy. Heads of industry in Mifflin County wanted an improved airport and the current Mifflin County Airport was organized as a municipal authority in 1964 and opened in 1966 with a paved runway and lights. Lanny was the manager when the original airport closed down and he, too, went to the new airport. Lanny resides in Milroy and helps with the monthly fly-in breakfasts.

With operations ceased, dissolution of the airport began in 1971 and was completed in 1973. The property was sold to James Knarr and Brown Rook. Knarr used the hangar for D.K. Hostetler Truck Bodies & Trailers and is still in existence today. A majority of the property was used for Brooknarr, a housing development.

Col. Hostetler retired from the U.S. Air Force in 1970 with 30 years of service. He served in the China, Burma, India Theater of War and was one of the last personnel to leave China before the Communist Party came to power. He died January 27, 2001.

Bill Sager also served in the China, Burma, India Theater of War and died in an airplane crash that he was piloting in Florida in 1987.

Honey Creek Inn, Reedsville

Honey Creek Inn, Reedsville, in 1966. From the postcard collection of Chris Kearns, Lewistown.

Honey Creek Inn interior, 1967 menu and business card courtesy of John Rodgers, of Reedsville, in 2009.

HONEY CREEK INN

STELLA JOHNSON, Proprietress

Route 322
Phone 196M

REEDSVILLE
PA.

Service and Quality Our Two Marked Features

Honey Creek Inn Menue - Reedsvil

Tuesday October 17, 1967

Appetizers
Fresh Shrimp Cocktail 80¢   Chilled Juice 20¢
Fruit Cup 20¢
Vegetable Soup Cup 15¢ Bowl 25¢

ALA CARTE
Broiled Sirloin Steak, Onion Rings...............3.50
Broiled T Bone Steak, Onion Rings...............3.25
Broiled Tenderloin Steak, Onion Rings..........3.25
Shore Platter, Lobster Tail........................4.50
Steamed Lobster Tail, Hot Butter..................4.00
Braised Shad Roe, Bacon Strip.....................3.00
Assorted Sea Food Platter..........................3.00
Fresh Shrimp Filled with Crab Meat..............2.00
Fried Oysters, Cocktail Sauce......................1.85
Breaded Fan Tail Shrimp, Hot Sauce...............1.75
2 Crab Patties, Tartar Sauce........................1.50
CHOICE OF 2 VEGETABLES   COFFEE OR TEA

SPECIAL
CREAMED HAM & CHICKEN ON TOAST
MASHED POTATOES, PEPPER SLAW.........90¢

DINNERS
Fruit Cup   Soup   or   Juice
Roast Prime Ribs of Beef Au Jus...............2.75
Grilled Smoked Ham Steak...........................1.75
Braised Calf Liver, Bacon Strip...................1.75
Breaded Veal Cutlet, Tomato Sauce...............1.65
Fried Young Country Chicken........................1.65
Broiled Salmon Steak, Parsley Butter............1.65
Chopped Steak...1.50
FILLED PEACH SALAD AND 2 VEGETABLES
Mashed Potatoes   French Fries
Apple Sauce   Whole Corn

Milroy area

This picture of the bank and post office in Milroy was submitted by Susan and Carl King, of Lewistown.

This picture of the Laurel Run Inn in Milroy was submitted by Susan and Carl King, of Lewistown.

Belleville

An old postcard, left, shows Main Street in downtown Belleville.

Gibboney's Drugstore, below, is packed with a variety of items in the building that now houses Victory Antiques.

The storefront is shown in the bottom photo.

Photos courtesy of Barb Harmon, of Belleville, in 2009.

Sperry New Holland

Susan and Carl King, of Lewistown, have a vast collection of local memorabilia from local businesses, including from Sperry New Holland, where Carl had been employed. Here's a closer look at some of their collection.

Ye Olde Canal Inn

By Sue Foltz
Lewistown

These pictures are of "Ye Olde Canal Inn," which was owned and operated by my grandparents, Harold and Blanche Gregg.

Back in the 1940s, the business was located in the Lewistown Narrows, where, in later years, Tony's Cottage Inn once was.

The business was a restaurant and bar, with cabins for rent, and was a popular spot for travelers. Note the signs stating, "Liquor, wines, mixed drinks, cabins," and the one that says, "Chicken dinners, 50 cents."

I love the old cars in the photos.

My grandparents later in life owned the Lewistown Block Co. (We could not find any pictures of this company.)

My grandparents had two children, a son, the late Howard Gregg, and a daughter, Donna (Gregg) Spickler, my mother. I never knew my grandfather, as he died of leukemia during my mother's senior year of high school. I have many great memories of my grandmother, until her death after a brave fight with melonoma cancer.

Matchbook memorabilia

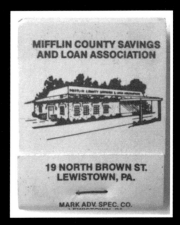

From Jane Mort

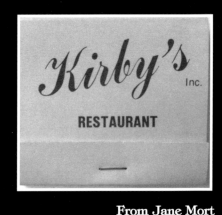

From Jane Mort

From John Rodgers

From Freda Richard

From Carrol "Sis" Norton

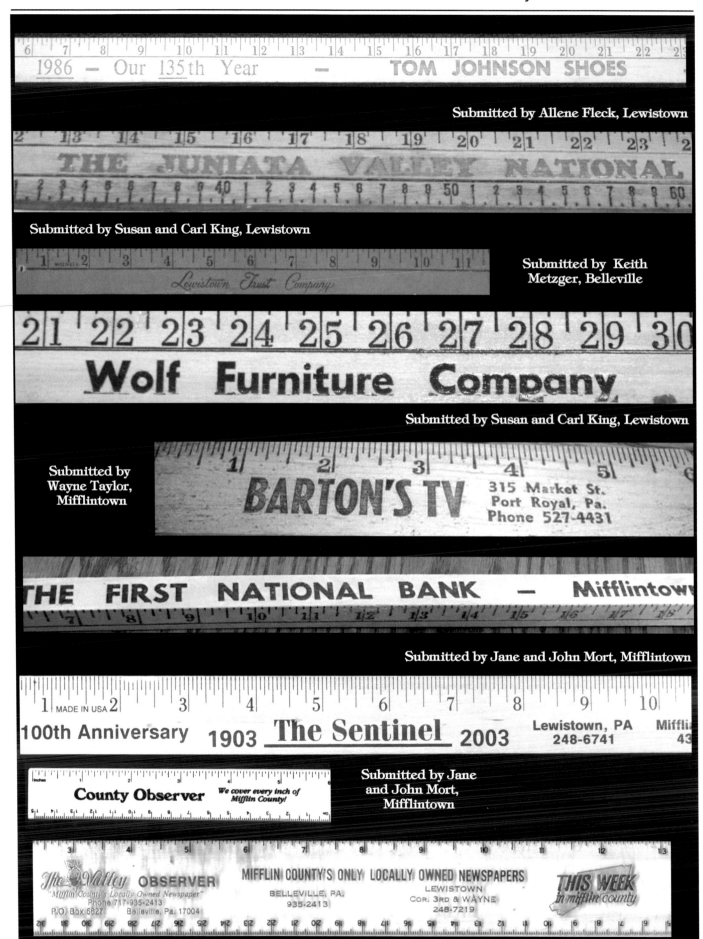

1986 – Our 135th Year – TOM JOHNSON SHOES

Submitted by Allene Fleck, Lewistown

THE JUNIATA VALLEY NATIONAL

Submitted by Susan and Carl King, Lewistown

Lewistown Trust Company

Submitted by Keith Metzger, Belleville

Wolf Furniture Company

Submitted by Susan and Carl King, Lewistown

Submitted by Wayne Taylor, Mifflintown

BARTON'S TV
315 Market St.
Port Royal, Pa.
Phone 527-4431

THE FIRST NATIONAL BANK – Mifflintown

Submitted by Jane and John Mort, Mifflintown

100th Anniversary 1903 The Sentinel 2003 Lewistown, PA 248-6741 Miffli 43

County Observer — We cover every inch of Mifflin County!

Submitted by Jane and John Mort, Mifflintown

The Valley OBSERVER
"Mifflin County's Locally Owned Newspaper"
Phone 717-935-2413
P.O. Box 5827 Belleville, Pa. 17004

MIFFLIN COUNTY'S ONLY LOCALLY OWNED NEWSPAPERS
BELLEVILLE, PA.
935-2413
LEWISTOWN
COR. 3RD & WAYNE
248-7219

THIS WEEK in mifflin county

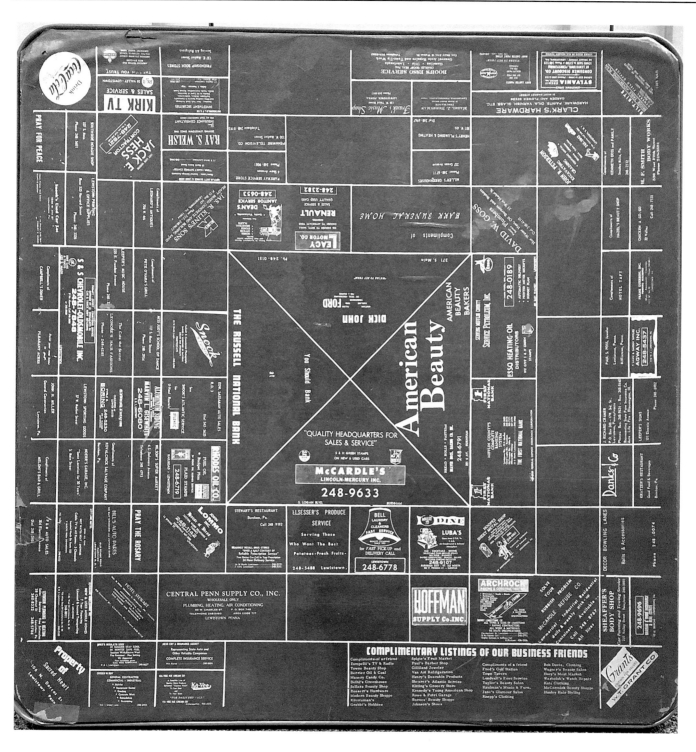

Tom Storm, of Lewistown, received this circa 1960 bridge table at a yard sale. It provides a snapshot of some of the businesses in the region at the time.

Juniata County

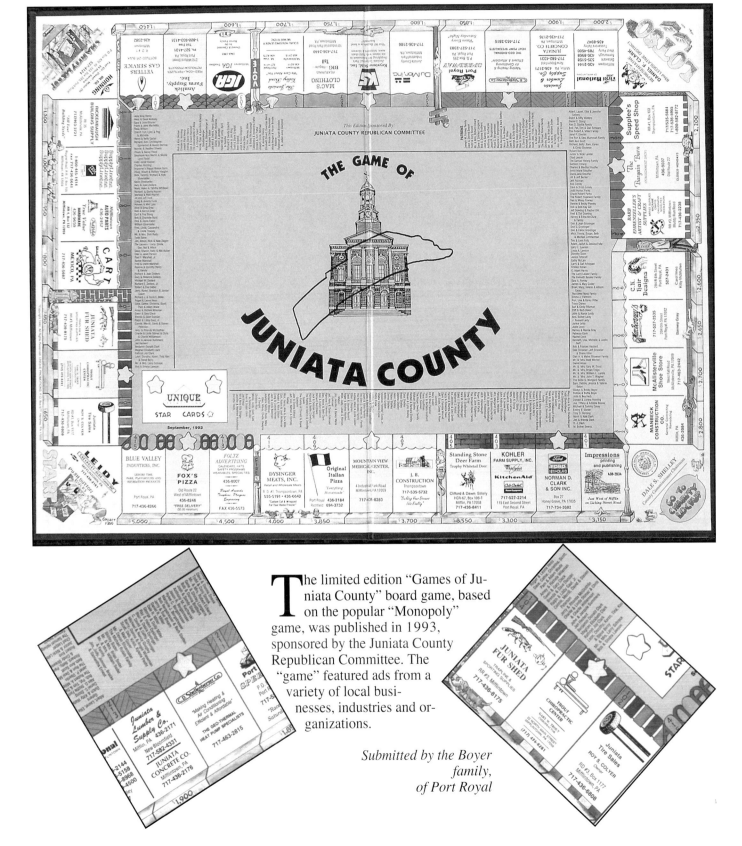

The limited edition "Games of Juniata County" board game, based on the popular "Monopoly" game, was published in 1993, sponsored by the Juniata County Republican Committee. The "game" featured ads from a variety of local businesses, industries and organizations.

Submitted by the Boyer family, of Port Royal

C.C. Markel Variety Store

1892

1932

Harold Lauver, of East Salem, submitted these photos of the C.C. Markel Variety Store in East Salem. The dates on the photos range from 1892 to 1936. Note the old bicycle on top of the porch in the 1932 picture above. In the photo at right of a shed at the back of the store, Markel can be seen at left, and the handles of a long row of mowers can be seen in the foreground.

1936

M.E. Sowers
Quality Cash Market

In Mifflintown

By Mary Berrier Hughes
Lewistown

M.E. Sowers Quality Cash Market, at 10 North Main Street, Mifflintown. The phone number was 60X. The proprietor was Melvin E. Sowers.

In the early days, his wife, Minnie, worked with him behind the cash register.

The store was known for quality meats, friendly service and home deliveries.

People could run a tab, and pay their bill when they got their checks at the beginning of the month.

I think the store closed in 1969, and M. Sowers had it for 49-plus years.

The M.E. Sowers Quality Cash Market in Mifflintown was owned by Mary Berrier Hughes' grandfather.

All photos for this story submitted by Wayne Taylor

Hertzler's Old Port Store, 1838-1913

Store opened when Old Port was St. Tammany's Town

Editor's note: This article originally appeared in "I Remember When ... II," a special section published by The Sentinel in 2009.

By Wayne E. Taylor
Mifflintown

I remember the store in Old Port. The village of Old Port is located at the intersection of Routes 75 and 333 in Turbett Township, Juniata County. Old Port was originally known as St. Tammany's Town, named by Lawrence King. The name of St. Tammany's Town first appeared on the tax lists in 1799 and in the same year appeared on a return on a petition in court.

Old Port, 1900

Hertzler's Old Port Store, 1838-1913

About 1833, the post office was established in the village and named Port Royal as a tribute to Lawrence King. St. Tammany's Town was much more important than its neighbor, Perrysville, before the canal and railroad were constructed. In 1847, the "Port Royal" post office was moved to the borough of Perrysville due to increased activity on the canal and railroad. The name Perrysville was already in use in Pennsylvania and it was not until 1874 that the borough appropriated the name of Port Royal. The Pennsylvania Railroad Co. changed the name of the station on Dec. 1, 1875. St. Tammany's Town eventually became known as Old Port.

Noah Hertzler and two of his brothers constructed a store and warehouse in the hamlet of St. Tammany's Town in 1838. In 1842, Noah built a stone house next to the store. Later, Noah became the sole owner of the enterprise and, in 1851, he built an addition to the structure. In 1902, J.D. Hertzler purchased the business from Noah's other heirs, and at that time it was said that it was the largest and finest general store, as well as the oldest, in Juniata County.

On the night of April 11, 1913, the

**Josh Ritzman and
Bernal Taylor**

structure was entirely consumed by flames, with a loss estimated at $15,000, with $6,750 covered by insurance. The stone house next door was badly scorched and blistered, as was the handsome brick residence of William Hertzler, Deputy Secretary of

the Commonwealth, which stands on the opposite side of the road.

A larger and more modern building was erected on the same site by the end of the year. The store remained in the Hertzler family until Dec. 11, 1929, when the stock, fixtures and store room were purchased by William R. Moyer, of Berrysburg, Dauphin County, from Noah and Elizabeth Hertzler. Noah was the grandson of the store's founder.

The store operated under the name of W.R. and M. Moyer. William died and eventually Mrs. Moyer sold the enterprise to Miles J. Heckendorn Jr., and his wife, Sara, on Aug. 19, 1946. On Jan. 26, 1949, the Heckendorns sold the store and house to Glen D. Kepner Sr., and his wife, S. Martha and Bernal E. Taylor, and his wife, Ruth.

The store was renamed the Old Port Trading Post, and this partnership lasted until Sept. 17, 1957, when the Taylors bought the business from the Kepners.

The Old Port Trading Post was a general store and sold just about anything that a person needed or desired. Groceries were the mainstay, but also available were shoes, boots, guns and hunting supplies, fishing supplies, bolts, nails, paints, clothing, sewing supplies, seasonal gifts — and the list goes on. Basically, we sold a little bit of everything. Credit was extended quite easily, and barter also was used, especially with eggs.

Tuesdays were a busy day at the store. The tractor and trailer from Harrisburg Groceries, which carried mostly Aunt Nellie's food products, arrived at about 11 o'clock. Each box and carton had to be checked in, marked with a price and placed on the shelves or in the back room.

We sold Juniata Ice Cream, which was produced in Mifflintown until that creamery went out of business, then we sold Sealtest products. We had one gas pump, from which we sold Atlantic gas; of course, gas was only 15 or 16 cents a gallon. A kerosene pump was located in the basement.

Most of our fresh meat products were bought at Barton's Meat Market, and usually we picked them up on Thursday so we would have a good supply of meat for the weekend.

In the early and mid-50s, most families made only one trip to the store per week, usually Friday or Saturday night, and the store would remain open until 9 o'clock. Those were normally the two busiest days and nights at the store. Families would buy their supplies to last for a week.

Many wives would send their husbands, or mothers would send their children with shopping lists, and we would fill their orders. Often people would call in their shopping lists for us to fill. We had to ask specific questions to make sure we placed the correct items in the orders.

We also delivered orders; once I got my driver's license, this became the fun part of working in the store. We delivered to Tuscarora, Van Dyke, Groninger Valley, Spruce Hill, Port Royal and all places in between. My favorite delivery was to Bill Landis, who lived on Mountain Road in Turbett Township, in the same house his grandson, Don

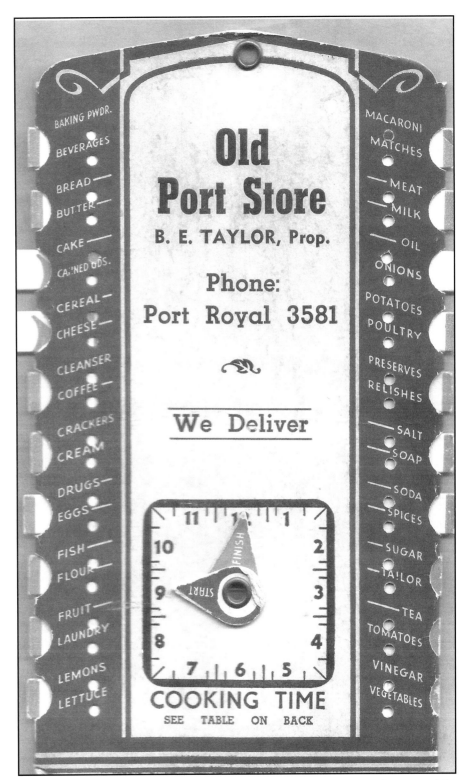

Bryner, now lives in.

When I left to make Bill's delivery, my mother would laugh and say that she would see me in a few hours. Bill worked on the railroad with my grandfather, J.W. "Brownie" McCachren. He was full of the most interesting stories. Bill's

grandson, Ronnie Fogelman, and I were the same age, and earlier we had been in the Boy Scouts together, and Bill always kept me informed about Ron's activities. Ron went on to become Gen. Ronald Fogelman.

The store served as a social center for many men until television began

Old Port Store, 1949-50

to keep the men at home during the evenings. The store served as a second home for these men. The men who gathered at the store were termed "loafers." During cold weather, the loafers sat around the floor stove register to keep warm. When the weather was warm, there was a permanent bench built between two porch posts on the south end of the porch and a movable bench placed against the building that served as the gathering spot for the loafers.

George Landis, Noah "Nook" Hertzler, Ross Weimer, John Yingst, Shelley Sowders, Charlie Koons, Ralph Landis, Lee Kerchner and Boots Smith were some of the men that I can remember spending evenings at the store. I can remember hearing Mrs. Landis and Mrs. Hertzler yelling at their husbands that it was time for them to come home. I just wish I had

written down some of the stories that they related on those nights.

Baseball played a huge role in my family, as my grandfathers, my dad and his brothers, my brother, cousins and I played for one of the Port Royal teams. My dad was manager of the Port Royal team in the Perry-Juniata League when he died in 1959. We had a slate board that we placed on the porch and wrote the time and location of our games to encourage fans to attend our games.

Hunting also was a popular activity involving the store. In the '50s, there weren't many deer in Juniata County, and after the first day of buck season, a gang of hunters would meet at the store early in the morning and stage deer drives on the Tuscarora Mountain or the Herringbone Ridge. Depending on my dad's work schedule, he might be able to go hunting on certain days,

and sometimes I would be able to go along. I never had a rifle, instead I carried my Winchester 16 gauge pump shotgun loaded with slugs or "punkin balls."

The McClures, Gilsons, Isenbergs, Kerlins, Landises and many others joined the Kepners and Taylors in pursuit of the white-tails. After a successful hunt, the deer would be butchered in the basement of the store.

Area hunters and sportsmen created the Tuscarora Valley Sportsmen Association that held its meetings at the store. In the second floor of the store, they constructed a 50-foot shooting range for 22 rifles. The range was set up diagonally from corner to corner. In the southwest corner, six railroad ties were stood on end to create a solid backstop. A steel plate was hung on the ties at an angle so that the spent lead would glance to the bottom of the steel plate and stick in the ties or fall harmlessly to the floor where a pile of sand had been dumped. In front of the ties was a pineboard backstop that held the targets.

My cousin, Skip Kepner, and I would collect the lead from the railroad ties and take it over to the house and melt the lead into sinkers to be used for fishing.

The shooting was very competitive, with groceries often being the prizes. The sportsmen's club also held outdoor shoots on the farm where Skip and Spence Kepner now live. One of the big events was the live pigeon shoot, which would not be allowed today. The pigeons would be caught in the barns throughout the valley and caged and fed until the Saturday of the shoot. A large hole was dug in the ground and the pigeons would be released from the hole on a given signal.

Clay birds and stationary targets for rifles were other events. Often the prizes were poultry, beef and pork products. The shoots were very popular and well attended.

Model cars were raced in the upper floor of the store. This was before remote cars. Instead, cables were attached to the cars and to a center support pole in the middle of the room. I was never allowed to attend these races, so my knowledge and memories of the races is very limited.

We boys took over the smaller room on the second floor of the store and turned it into a ping pong or table tennis room. The games would go on until late at night.

The most unusual visitor that came into the Old Port Store was this part-white young buck.

The most unusual visitor, not really a customer, that came into the store was a part-white buck fawn. The kids who lived in the old stone house on the McClure farm (originally Rice's Tavern) adopted this young deer. He followed those kids everywhere, and, of course, to the store and into it. The problem arose when he developed a "sweet tooth" and loved candy and chips, and he would head for those immediately. The young buck loved to have his ears and buttons rubbed. Eventually, the part-white buck was taken to a game farm.

Sadly, on July 4, 1959, my father, Bernal, at the age of 41, died of a cerebral hemorrhage. My mother kept a bulletin board behind the counter where she placed the school pictures of the kids who came into the store. I still have some of those pictures: the Ritzman girls, the Hower girls, the Yoders, the Kints, Henrys, Bakers, Bartons, Groningers, McClures, Kerlins, Brynes, Werts, Walters, Robinsons, and many of my cousins. I know I missed some names; I apologize for those omissions.

Two events occurred in 1968 that changed the business atmosphere in Old Port and Port Royal. Tuscarora Valley High School closed its doors and the students were bused to Mifflintown to Juniata Joint, which is now Juniata High School. The IGA Store moved into Mifflintown, spelling doom to all the small stores in the area.

Although the Old Port Store closed in late 1970, the memories of the good people that I met in those years will never be forgotten. It's always a thrill when I meet some of these old friends and have the opportunity to talk about the good old days at Old Port. Today, the building houses St. John's Garage, owned and operated by Francis St. John since 1981.

The Old Port Store closed in late 1970, and Francis St. John located a garage in the building in 1981.

'The Store' in East Waterford

Editor's note: This article originally appeared in "I Remember When ... II," a special section published by The Sentinel in 2009. It was written by the late Paula Diven, of Honey Grove.

Early Sunday morning of Memorial Day weekend, my husband walked in the door and said, "Bad news, the store burned last night."

I didn't have to ask, "What store?" because there was only one as far as the people of East Waterford were concerned.

Long's Store loomed large in the lives of everyone around here. From resident to weekend camper, "the store" was there for our needs.

If you needed a screw for a weekend project, you went to "the store."

If you needed a part to fix the plumbing, you went to "the store."

If you wanted the freshest hamburger in the world, you went over and got ground beef that you were certain was ground that day. Sometimes you even watched as it was ground.

If you needed a garbage can or a can opener, you could get it at "Denny's."

As I processed the news, I wanted to cry. As people asked us about it later in the day, I couldn't keep the tears from falling. The store was so much a part of our lives. Harry and I have been married for almost 40 years and some of my first memories of coming to this area have to do with "the store."

When we were first married, we lived in Port Royal and we came up to visit Harry's parents on weekends. One of the first things his mother would do was to send him to "Bub's" to get a yeast cake for homemade bread. If she needed more, she would give us a list and tell us to put it on the slip. In an old fashioned file box

Sentinel archives

Long's Community Store, East Waterford, before the 2009 fire.

behind the counter, the owner, Bob Long, kept a running tally of purchases for local customers. The same box was behind the counter when the store burned on Sunday morning. One of the things I asked my husband was, "Did you have a slip when the store burned?" I didn't want to owe our old friend.

You see, over the years, the owners had become our friends. When Christmas or birthdays came around, I would simply go to "the store" and ask what Harry wanted. If Denny didn't know, he soon found out and then reported to me. I would then proceed to order it from him. I never had to worry if it would fit. One year it was a muzzle loader, the next a scope for his .30-30, or maybe, a much coveted pistol. Arrangements would be made

for another friend to pick up the item and the surprise was complete.

When hunting season came, there was only one place to get your license; Long's Store. Denny always had one person working full-time filling out the paperwork for hunters who would be lined up at the glass display case trading stories of past hunts. Nobody was in a hurry. Everyone loved visiting and sharing memories while they waited. The day before deer season was the only day that "the store" was opened on Sunday. There was always the ritual trip to Long's for candy bars to take to the woods or peanuts for card playing. It didn't matter how much you already had, it was just part of the tradition.

Butcher day was another day when a trip to Long's was in order. Rolls for lunch or sausage casings for stuffing, someone always had to go to Long's. We called it the East Waterford Wal-Mart. It seemed that there wasn't anything Denny didn't have. A few times we stumped him and he would look in the books behind the old roll top desk and say, "I can order it and have it here by Wednesday."

He was never too busy to serve a customer. Like his father before him, he was never too busy to trade jokes or friendly barbs, either. He knew local people and their history. He shared in our lives providing lunchmeat for funerals and coffee for local emergencies.

Local events like the fireman's carnival or the local Fourth of July celebration got their supplies from one source. Long's Store always came up with the stuff of which our celebrations were made. From chicken to watermelon, "the store" provided it all. The local Christian camp where my husband works had a weekly order delivered to Long's every summer. Denny just left it on the dock and the staff made a trip to pick it up at an appointed time each Thursday.

Odd things came out of the basement or upstairs of the store when you least expected it. Need a smoothing trowel? "I think there might be one upstairs," he would say and disappear to emerge a few minutes later with one in hand.

No matter that the price tag was still from the '50s or '60s, that was still the price.

Need chain for a swing or other project? Lay it out on the floor and measure by the floor tiles. If you were a local, you might have to do this for yourself while he served someone else and he always trusted your word.

Need a few nails? Look back in the bins, measure them out, weigh them, and tell the girls the price when you come up to the counter.

A gallon of gas for the mower? "How much did you get?"

"The store" was full of experiences like that from times long gone in our hustle, bustle world.

A few minutes after I heard the news, I telephoned my daughter in

Sentinel archives

Long's Store, a long-time landmark in East Waterford

Georgia. You see, Long's Store was a big part of her growing up. She visited Santa there when she was a little girl. She and Grandpa went to the store for tools and ice cream. Her first solo trips after she learned to drive were to the store because the back roads were relatively safe and she didn't have to venture out on the highway if she went in the back way.

She turned to her urban-born husband and told him to cherish his Long's Store hat because he may never get another. She said part of her childhood was gone and she was right.

Where else could you buy groceries with trophy bucks staring down at you from the wall? Where else could you walk to the back of the store and interrupt the store owner doing his books to ask if he was going to get reindeer droppings (aka chocolate creme drops) for Christmas stockings? Where else could you dip into the same case where you got your ice cream when you were a child and hand a cone off to the next generation? Where else could you show your grandchildren a real stuffed fox? Where else could you walk in after many a year's absence and find things in the same place they were when you left?

Long's Store was not your run-of-the-mill convenience store for bread, milk and overpriced snack foods. As a matter of fact, the prices were pretty good for a country store. Many cabin owners came there to buy rather than transfer goods from home.

To say that East Waterford would miss the store if Denny doesn't rebuild would be an understatement. The store was the center of the community. It was the heartbeat of the town. If someone died, you called the store. They knew the arrangements before they came out in the paper. Sometimes, they even knew what kinds of dishes the ladies from the area were making to take to the family.

Long's Store served our community in more ways than can be printed on paper. Its loss is more than an inconvenience. It can never be duplicated or totally replaced. It's a given that we want our store back.

The oldest member of our community has died and we can't go to "the store" to get anything to help the hurt.

• • •

Editor's note: The following article orignally appeared in The Sentinel's Juniata County Progress Edition in October 2010. It is edited for space.

By Marjorie Stromberg
The Sentinel

Some might believe that the story of Long's Community Store is a perfect example of a community coming together to put back a missing

Sentinel archives

Long's Community Store, 2010

piece of a puzzle.

After a long-standing neighborhood staple was destroyed last year following an accident, many came forward with hope, support and determination, and the store was rebuilt. Now, Long's is up and running, it offers more of a selection, and plans to serve the community for years to come.

Dennis Long, who owns the East Waterford store with his wife Belinda, said it seemed like the customers were waiting patiently for the store to open again, and now they're returning.

And with the rebuild came some expansion, he said.

The store's frozen food capacity has doubled, Long said. Additionally, there are a variety of new grocery items, new items in the deli case, and now the store offers freshly-made hoagies, sandwiches and salads, he said.

Also, another meat case was added, so there is a case for meat, and a separate one for deli, Long said.

The new items were added because the store now has more room, Long said. Shelf space increased by more than 250 feet, and some additional square footage was added.

The old store, which was two stories, occupied approximately 4,000 square feet of retail space, Long said. The new building, which is one story, occupies about 4,100.

During the rebuild, the store was designed so that there could be more of a selection, he said.

Also, builders tried to be as energy-efficient as possible in such areas as refrigeration and insulation, Long said, which will help the store function efficiently in the future.

The store has gotten a lot of encouraging feedback since its reopening, he said. Community members have said they think the store looks nice, and have commented on the lighting and how bright it is, he said.

"It's all been positive," he said.

Long said the store plans to continue to serve the community now, and in years to come, by listening to customer feedback and trying to carry new items if a customer requests them.

The Longs have owned the store since 1987 when they purchased it from Dennis' parents, R.F. and Doris Long, who had purchased it in 1958.

Hotel remembered in book

Editor's note: This article originally appeared in The Sentinel on August 12, 2017.

By Jane Cannon Mort
The Sentinel

It was beautiful with its high ceilings and fancy walnut woodwork. Especially the huge bar with its magnificent mirror behind it. That's how Edwina "Eddie" Johnson Bryner remembers the Hotel Royal.

Kay Crimmel Leach remembers watching movies there when she was about 5 years old.

Wayne Taylor can name a long list of childhood friends who played Cowboys and Indians there in the 1950s.

Today, there's an empty lot at the corner of Milford and Second streets in Port Royal, where the three-story brick Hotel Royal stood until it was demolished in February.

There was heartbreak among those who grew up around the old hotel when the bricks and dust settled, but their memories will be kept alive forever in a new book by Wayne Taylor. "Hotel Royal 1902-2017" is now available for purchase.

"I grew up in Port Royal," Taylor said, earlier this month, just after picking up the book from the printer.

"The Hotel Royal was always a mainstay in our town. Like everyone else, I was sorry to see it go," he said. "Lots of people had questions about it, so I started to dig in and get some answers."

Taylor was the right person for the job. He taught history in Juniata County schools for more than 30 years, and authored a three-book series of historical fiction — "Hope on the Tuscarora," Hope Rekindled" and "Across Five Valleys," tracing local history from the time of the French and Indian War to the Civil War.

He is also the author of "The Baseball Era of Fred Frankhouse," a biography of Port Royal's famed major

Sentinel archives courtesy Wayne Taylor

The Hotel Royal
Port Royal

leaguer, and he assisted with the production of a history book of the town, published during its bicentennial.

The demolition of the building in February prompted Taylor to move on a project he had been researching and contemplating for a number of years.

"I talked to people who gave me stories about what they remembered," Taylor said. "The bad thing was so many people that I needed to talk to are no longer with us."

Relying on those memories, as well as stories from Juniata County and Harrisburg newspapers, Taylor pieced together the history of the Hotel Royal. He said the majority of the vintage photos in the book are from the collection of D. Leon Kepner, and color photos of the razing of the hotel are courtesy of Donna L. Brothers, Sherry Losch and Paul Williams.

In the book, Taylor offers factual information, such as the names of the various owners and the dates events occurred, and puts it all into historical

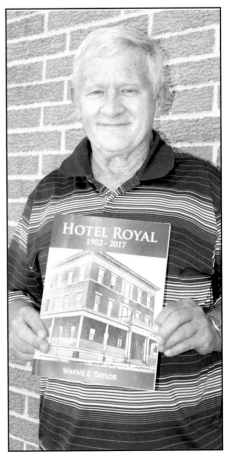

Sentinel archives

perspective. The book begins with Taylor stating his intent to "explain why this structure fell into disuse as a hotel and disrepair after playing a major role in Port Royal's history for nearly as century."

He identifies 11 factors that he believes contributed to the failure and demise of the Hotel Royal, including absentee owners, inconsistent proprietors and small clientele due to the sparse population in the area. Other factors were more political in nature, such as the loss of the hotel's liquor license at various times and Prohibition itself.

The book looks at the local railroads and how their decline affected the hotel, and even inspects the effect of the influenza epidemic of 1918-19 had on the business.

Additional factors Taylor cites as hindering the success of the hotel were more global: the United States entry into World War I in 1917, the Great Depression in 1929, and the U.S. involvement in World War II.

• • •

One of author Wayne Taylor's favorite photos of the Hotel Royal shows the grassy bank, below, which indicates that the photo was taken in 1906, before the construction of the East and West Stations. In his book,

The Hotel Royal was situated near the railroad station in the town.

Taylor points out that the hotel was one of the businesses in the town that benefitted tremendously from the annual Juniata County Fair.

"Some people who traveled a distance to attend the fair would reserve rooms at the hotel because all Pennsylvania Railroad traffic disembarked almost on the front steps of the hotel. The rooms and dining area were filled to overflowing during the fair. The Hotel Royal was also a quieter place to obtain a nice meal, away from the hustle and bustle of the fairgrounds,"

the book states.

In addition, "The Tuscarora Railroad unloaded most of its fair travelers at the Sixth Street entrance to the fairgrounds, although numerous men would continue to the end of the line right across from the Hotel Royal, where they could wet their whistle before taking in the sights and sounds of the fair."

The grassy area was said to be a gathering place for those men who may have not made it as far as the fairgrounds.

The food store sign is a part of the collection of old signs and photos owned by Frank and Kirk Stevens and displayed at Steven Auctioneering on Market Street in Lewistown. It appears to be the same sign on the building in Port Royal that housed Foltz's Community Pure Food Store. The photo shows the store in about 1950, when it operated as a grocery store by Charles Foltz. The photo was submitted by Wayne Taylor, of Mifflintown.

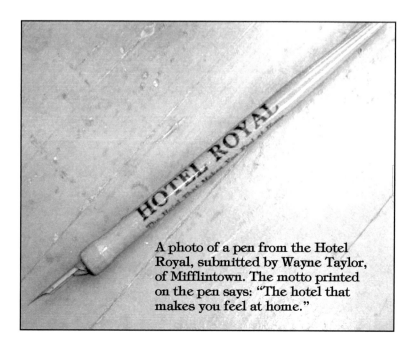

A photo of a pen from the Hotel Royal, submitted by Wayne Taylor, of Mifflintown. The motto printed on the pen says: "The hotel that makes you feel at home."

Photos submitted by Wayne Taylor, Mifflintown

Photo submitted by Wayne Taylor, Mifflintown

Businesses that line the street in the borough of Mifflin include Bratton's Restaurant and E.M. Guss and Sons Hardware Store.

A photo of a postcard submitted by Wayne Taylor, of Mifflintown, shows the interior and exterior of Zimmie's Diner, formerly located in Mifflintown.

In Mifflintown

Photos courtesy of the Juniata County Historical Society

The former William Banks Hotel once housed the Juniata County Library and is now owned by attorney Andrew Winder, whose office is located in the building at the corner of Main and Lemon streets in Mifflintown.

The former Snyder Furniture store at the corner of North Main and Orange streets in Mifflintown.

Memory Lane, Mifflintown

Editor's note: This article originally appeared in "I Remember When ... II," a special section published by The Sentinel in 2009.

By Sondra Woodling
Mifflintown

I remember when, in Mifflintown, on Main Street, going west:

The front door to the First National Bank was on the corner.

Zimmie's Restaurant — Violet and Les Zimmerman

Banks Drug Store (upstairs was the telephone company with operators who connected your calls)

Quality Cash Grocery — Melvin Sowers

Milliken's Restaurant — Gerry and Les

Simonton's Hardware — Charlie

Gordon's Department Store (after moving from Bridge Street)

Esther Lauver's Beauty Shop

A&P Store, on the corner of Orange and Main streets

Cup Ford Auto Garage (later Elmer Lauver)

Frank Hostler's gas station

Dr. Banks

Dr. Sausser

The library was in the hotel

Main Street going east:

Post office on the corner

Goshen's Men's Store — later Buster Brown Shoes

Newspaper — bookstore

Minick's Barber Shop

Telephone company

Gulf Gas Station

Mifflin Creamery

Tuscarora Junior High School was Juniata Joint High School

Daup's Garage — Zimmie's Diner

Two grocery stores — A&P and IGA — Also a Ben Franklin

Western Auto

Mifflintown Pharmacy

Shoffstall's Restaurant at the blink-

The inside and outside of Chapple's Restaurant are preserved in these photos submitted in 2009 by Sondra Woodling, of Mifflintown.

ing light

Bridge Street toward Mifflin:

George and Bea's Hoagie Shop

Beward's Drug Store

Gordon's Department Store

Henry's Hardware and Furniture

Lepperts 5&10

Mac's Clothing

Brown's Funeral Home — now run by Dan Brown

Another garage

And at the end of Front Street, Potter's Bus Garage

Across the bridge:

Bratton's Restaurant

Movie theater

Shiveley's Department Store

Guss Hardware

Leister's Grocery

Mahlon Guss Drug Store

Walter's Restaurant, where Juniata Garment is now

Bridge Street:

Juniata Valley Bank had a driver-thru

Ray Shirk's Grocery, with home delivery

Across the street was the fire company; now it is up the street.

Dick Harry's Grocery

Bowling alley — the boys were the pin setters

Frys had a greenhouse on North Street

Benners had a greenhouse behind Swayer Avenue

Kauffman's Dairy was on Sixth Street

S. Wayde Norris Plumbing and Heating, rear of Third Street

Terry Quay had a greenhouse on

Cross Street

Dr. Stratford — Third Street

Audrey's Beauty Shop — Third Street

Mifflin Dry Cleaners — Seventh Street

Ona Miller's Grocery on Sixth Street

Going west on Old Route 22:

Dwason's Sunoco Station

Grey Switzer's Chevrolet Garage

Atlantic and Texaco stations

As You Like It Cottages and Motel

Anion Mingle's Garage — later Lauver's

Doc Ryner's little store at Cuba Mills

Don's Fruit Market — now Dollar Daze

Juniata Tribune — now Juniata Sentinel

Paul Beale's Custard Stand — now Rhonda's

Homer Smith's Chrysler Garage

Chevron Gas Station — Cameo Kitchen there now

Orwig's Greenhouse — now Treaster's

Niman's junkyard

I also remember when they built the Midway Drive-In across from Chapple's Restaurant and Motel, which my father, Thomas, built. It was opened in 1949, and operated by him and my mother, Gert. I also remember my dad pushing the snow off the pond behind the restaurant so people could skate there in the winter.

Twin Kiss Custard Stand

Ira and Flossie Smith rented rooms at Pinehurst

Elsie Clouser's William Penn Bar and Grille

Terrace Gardens

Wildwood Restaurant — If I keep going, we'll be in Lewistown, and that's another story

This photo of Heck's Store in Mifflintown was among a number of images on glass plates that the late Dick Cramer, of Belleville, acquired when he was a youth, from his father, Crawford Cramer, of Lewistown. The plates originated with a Mr. Sowers, a Juniata County photographer. The plates, later owned by Cramer, contain images shot in Juniata County from 1899 to 1912. Many of the photographs include images of Cramer's grandfather and great-grandparents, who lived in Juniata County. Some of the images were first published in "I Remember When ... II," a special section printed by The Sentinel in 2009.

Juniata Valley businesses through the decades

1800s

1894:

"A trading post was established here (Lewistown) one hundred and forty years ago, from which the town grew."

"... business places are varied enough to supply all ordinary demands, while the tri-weekly market furnishes an abundance of choice products from the fruitful agricultural district of the county."

ROBERT H. MONTGOMERY, Jr.,

Manufacturer of

BUGGIES,

CARRIAGES,

Spring Wagons,

AND

VEHICLES OF EVERY DESCRIPTION

Constantly on hand, at the

Junction of Third and Valley Streets,

LEWISTOWN, PA.

———·:·———

☞ **REPAIRING**

of all kinds promptly attended to.

1870

Stoves! Stoves!!

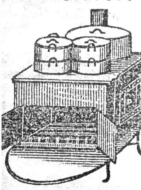

We have now on hand the most extensive assortment of STOVES ever offered for sale in this county, and at LOW PRICES. We have on hand the following kind of Cooking Stoves, viz: LAUBACH, 2 sizes, at $25 and $30; STAR, two sizes, at $20 and $25; COMPLETE COOK. 1 size, $13.50; FARMER, 1 size. We have also Airtight Parlor Stoves, a great variety of splendid patterns, some as low as $6; Coal Stoves, 4 sizes, some as low as $2.50; Nine Plate Stoves, 22 to 28 inches, some with BOILER TOPS; and Cylinder Coal Stoves, for cooking.

F. J. HOFFMAN.

Lewistown, Sept. 16, 1848—tf

1848

MILL FOR RENT.

WILL be rented by public outcry, on **SATURDAY, Dec. 23, 1848**, on the premises, for one or more years from the first day of April next, that desirable property known as **"STRODES MILLS,"** situate in Granville township, Mifflin county. The conditions will be made known on the day, and attendance given by

THE HEIRS OF A. STRODE.

December 2, 1848—td.

Store Stand and Grist Mill FOR RENT.

THE valuable *Store Stand* and *Grist Mills*, generally known as the Brown's Mills property, situate in Mifflin county, about 5 miles of Lewistown, are offered for rent. The

1848

1894

J. B. SELHEIMER'S
HARDWARE STORE,

Founded 1848, by the Late

N. E. COR. PUBLIC SQUARE.

Always a Full and Complete Line of

Hardware, Stoves,
Heaters, Ranges,
Oils, Paints,
Sporting Goods,
Wall Paper,
Tinware, &c.

Col. JNO. B. SELHEIMER.

Hardware Supplies for Furnaces. Mills, and other Industries a Specialty.

W. S. MAYES,

Plumber and Gasfitter, Steam and Hot Water Contractor.

Estimates Furnished.

All Work Guaranteed.

Agent for the Boynton Steam and Hot Water Systems of Heating.

N. MAIN STREET.
OPP. COURT HOUSE.

Lewistown, Pa.

1894:

"Do not forget the advertisers in this book. They are enterprising and fair dealing, they have shown a disposition to aid in advancing the interests of Lewistown, and deserve a liberal patronage one and all."

1909:

"The merchandising business has always been progressive and so well managed that financial failures among its regular merchants have been exceptionally few. One business has been conducted in the same name for more than 80 years, and others 60 to 70 years. A Merchants Association with a successful history was organized a few years ago."

"The mercantile business of the town is active and progressive. The stores compare well with those of much larger towns, and patronage of them is generous. There are large and modernly-managed and equipped department stores, and many establishments devoted to special lines."

OUR

SODA FOUNTAIN

Has been in readiness for patronage all winter long. If It gets too cold for the cold drinks you will always find the finest

HOT CHOCOLATE AND BOUILLON
at our Fountain

D. DUGHI & SON

J. H. FRETZ

Successor to W. H. Felix

FUNERAL DIRECTOR AND EMBALMER

AUTOMOBILE

AMBULANCE SERVICE

Cor. Valley and Dorcas Streets
Both Phones

1916

Wm. H. Wren   W. F. Eckbert, Jr.

FOR SALE

Matthew Kennedy property adjoining Shed Hawke at Mt. Rock. Owner is leaving town. This is a real bargain.

WREN & ECKBERT, Agts.

7 West Monument Square
LEWISTOWN, PENNA.

MID-WINTER

Have you Coal, Flour, Fee & International Stock Fee on hand? We have it!

LOGAN FLOUR MILL

THE BANK OF LIFE

You cannot both spend and save—save a little—forty years from now—a little—comes in handy—save a little.
AND NO WORRY

THE MIFFLIN COUNTY NATIONAL BANK

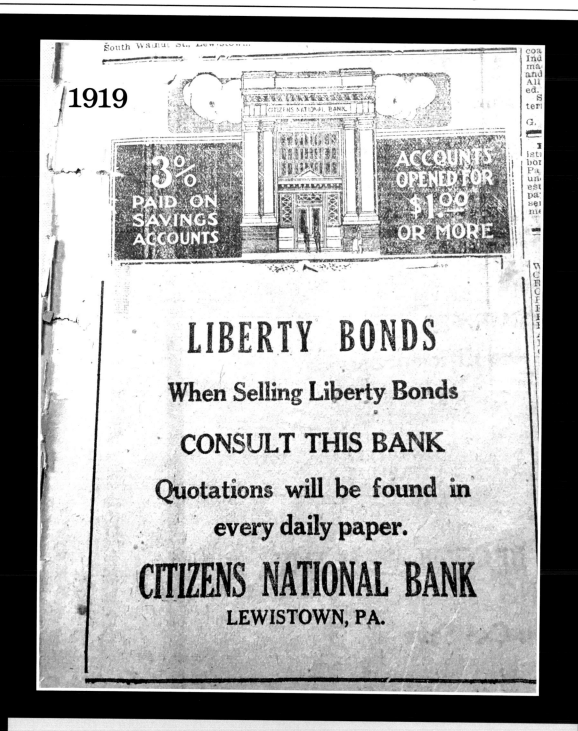

1919

South Walnut St., Lewistown.

CITIZENS NATIONAL BANK

3% PAID ON SAVINGS ACCOUNTS

ACCOUNTS OPENED FOR $1.00 OR MORE

LIBERTY BONDS

When Selling Liberty Bonds

CONSULT THIS BANK

Quotations will be found in every daily paper.

CITIZENS NATIONAL BANK
LEWISTOWN, PA.

1909:

"Lewistown has large wholesale grocery establishments and considerable wholesale business is also done in confectionery, tobacco, fruits and produce, &c."

"The professions are represented by men of ability and reputation."

"The town has first-class, modernly-equipped hotels and well-kept cafes."

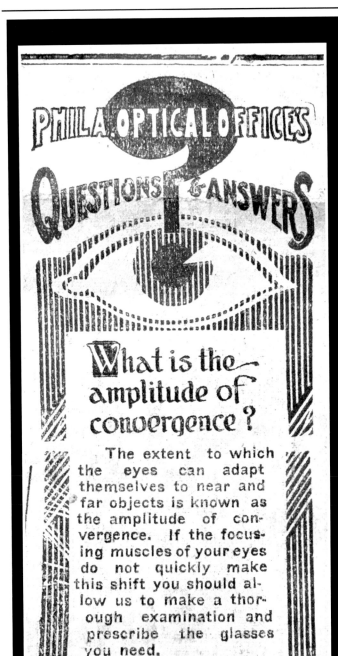

1919

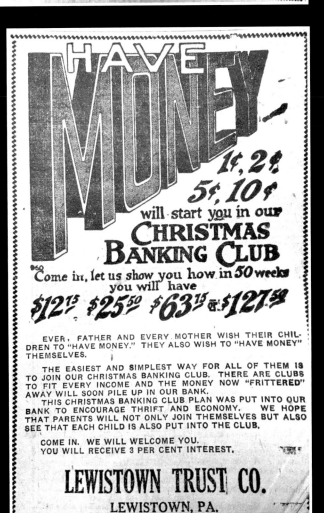

1920s

A hat that was thought very charming in 1824

Women who demand the best in millinery and yet who do not wish to pay exorbitant prices have come to learn that this is the shop of exclusive, fashionable models where prices are reasonable.

"Delightfully Different"

Model Hat Shoppe

30 Valley St.

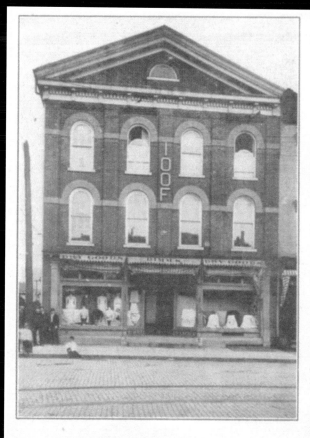

Lewistown Odd Fellows' Home

1925

"Frequently, the statement has been made without contradiction, that the commercial importance of a city is always reflected by the character and appearance of its retail stores.

"Should this be true, and it unquestionably is, Lewistown stands in the forefront of Pennsylvania cities, of no where in cities of Lewistown's size, and few of the larger communities, can finer stores be found. Visitors to Lewistown emphasize this almost every day, so it is not a mere boast.

"An array of stores that stand out prominently in appearance and in the quality of goods they carry cannot help but reflect on the prosperity of a community, and most of all it means business."

SALES AGENTS UNITED CIGAR STORES

LEWISTOWN NEWS CO.

KOPLOVITZ BROS., Proprietors

Cigars, Cigarettes, Tobacco, Smokers' Supplies, Magazines, Toys, OFFICE EQUIPMENT, Sporting Goods, Cameras, Newspapers, Stationery, Novelties

142 E. Market St.

1925

"Most of the larger stores have been built up from small beginnings; they have served the people faithfully and honestly for many generations, and, in turn, the patronage they have won has been reflected in their expansion and in the growth and development of the city itself."

1925

"One may travel for miles, for instance, and not find a line of such beautiful store fronts as are to be seen on Market Street. Moreover, the business district is no longer a strict Market Street proposition. Valley, South Main, Chestnut and other streets are blossoming forth into business streets."

Bell Phone
Residence—430-W
Office—173-W

RALPH BARCHUS
FUNERAL DIRECTOR

129 Valley St.   Lewistown, Pa.

EXPERT REPAIRING   ACCESSORIES AND SUPPLIES

J. Ralph McCook
THE MOTORCYCLE MAN

Distributor of

INDIAN MOTOCYCLES, TRUCKS, TIRES, RADIOS AND OILZUM MOTOR OILS

ESTABLISHED 1913

351 S. Main Street

LEWISTOWN, PA.

1925

"There is something about the mercantile life of Lewistown which has made it a great contributing factor to the growth of the city commercially, as well as financially, and the retail stores have not only been able to supply the needs of the citizens of Lewistown — men, women and children — but have also been the means of making the city a more and more satisfactory shopping center for the entire Juniata Valley."

COMPLIMENTS OF

The

Pallas

Restaurant

West Monument Square

1925

DRUG STORE SERVICE THAT WILL PLEASE YOU

Household Remedies—For Quick Relief
Sick Room Supplies that Aid Recovery
Hot Water Bottles, Fountain Syringes, Etc.
when needed

System Tonic Tones You Up. Makes Red Blood—$1.00 and Keep Well

Home Town Stationery—Tablets 15c, Envelopes 15c
Pens, Pencils, Inks, Etc.

Highest Grade Chocolates—90c to $1.20 a pound
Good Smokes at the right price

HERE YOU ARE—"WISTO"

For the thirsty, deliciousness for all. "Wisto," the wonder drink that athletes endorse, that wise business men enjoy—that everyone welcomes for its simple, pure wholesomeness—at all fountains—ask till they get it at—5c.

For Coughs, Throat and Bronchial troubles get One Day Cough Remedy—30, 60c, and $1.00. Everything usually carried in a Drug Store

First Aid Station

Get your Drugs, Medicine, and Rubber Goods at

EBY'S DRUG STORE

51 W. Market St.

Lewistown, Pa.   Opposite New Post Office Site

A Real Bakery

It has been twenty years since we decided that Lewistown should have a real Bakery. With this thought ever in mind, we have spared no expense in the improvement of our building or in the purchase of improved machinery in order to make the best bread and cakes possible. We have a Bakery that is really sanitary, good light and ventilation, and all modern equipment. Our modern methods, best materials, and first class workmen assure you of the best money can buy in our line. We extend you all a cordial invitation to visit our plant and see how quality bread and cakes are made.

Yours for Quality and Service

Letterman Bros.

44 Valley St.

1925

"The mercantile business of the town is conducted by active, enterprising men, and the line of stores compares favorably with those found in much larger towns. The needs of the consumers are well provided at home, leaving little necessity for outside shopping. The borough also has several large wholesale establishments."

1925

Old Home and McMeen's

JUNE 29th to JULY 4th, 1925

We believe that stores like this one owe something to the public beyond the mere gathering and selling of merchandise. In the old days the shopper had to have a good bit of Yankee shrewdness, had to know whether things were good or clever shams—or else she paid the penalty of buying trash. We believe that the big store of to-day has no business selling poor goods, no matter whether the buyer has discerning judgment or not.

We believe it is the duty of a store to make sure its goods are worthy before they reach its counters. We have carried this principle to the extreme, perhaps. Few stores are as careful that "wool" shall mean all wool; that toilet and remedial preparations shall answer every chemical test of excellence and purity, that clothing shall be made as well inside where it does not show, as it is outside where it does show. These things are carried to extremes here. Makers still tell us that we are foolishly careful; that our care is useless; that the public does not appreciate the difference

between the best and the "almost as good;" that we might just as well take the little extra profit that comes from selling the second grade.

But we know that our care is appreciated. We know that people everywhere have learned that buying here is saving; that they can depend on whatever comes from McMeen's store; that the McMeen standard means something. In this respect we are old fashioned and we most cordially invite all of our patrons of former years as well

as of the present to make McMeen's their headquarters during Old Home Week. Renew old acquaintences in our large and roomy aisles. Allow our loyal and courteous business associates to take care of your packages. Feel free to use our Telephone or to ask us for any information concerning our own store or the activities of Old Home Week. We assure you that any assistance which we might be privileged to render to visitors in Lewistown during this occasion by way of helping them to get acquainted or renew acquaintanceship with former friends or relatives will indeed, be a great pleasure to us.

E. E. McMEEN & CO.
THE BIG BUSY STORE IN THE HEART OF LEWISTOWN

1930

"By 1830 (Lewistown's) population had grown to 1,497. Brick and stone dwellings replaced the original cabins, and Market Street assumed an air of urban prosperity."

Among the 38 original subscribers to Bell Telephone in Mifflin County on June 7, 1883, were: Wian & Roundtree, National Hotel, Selheimer Hardware, Henderson (grocer), Russell Bank, Mifflin County National Bank, Franciscus Hardware, Hoffman Sons, Frysinger Book Store, Free Press, McClintic Furniture, Muthersbaugh, Felix Furniture, Goodhart & Houtz, Martin (druggist), Democrat and Sentinel.

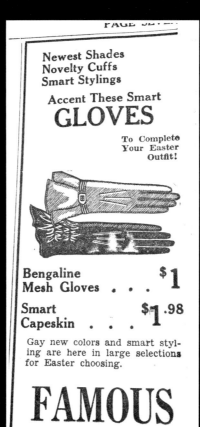

Newest Shades
Novelty Cuffs
Smart Stylings

Accent These Smart
GLOVES

To Complete
Your Easter
Outfit!

Bengaline
Mesh Gloves . . . **$1**

Smart
Capeskin . . . **$1.98**

Gay new colors and smart styling are here in large selections for Easter choosing.

FAMOUS

DANCE
TONITE
To The
Rayoneers
Orchestra
One of the Best
Beer, Light Wines and
Liquor
LOG CABIN INN

1936

1936

1945

Retail outlets in Lewistown on Oct. 1, 1945:

- 14 automobile agencies and garages
- 10 automobile supply stores
- 3 bakeries
- 16 beauty shops
- 5 building supply companies
- 4 cleaners and dryers
- 6 coal dealers
- 6 confectionery stores
- 4 dairies
- 3 department stores
- 5 drug stores
- 11 electrical equipment stores
- 2 farm equipment stores
- 4 Five cent to a dollar stores
- 3 florists
- 9 furniture stores
- 28 grocery stores
- 4 hardware stores
- 2 ice dealers
- 7 jewelry stores
- 2 laundries
- 3 magazine stores
- 6 meat markets
- 6 men's clothing stores
- 2 millinery shops
- 3 photograph studios
- 31 restaurants
- 7 shoe stores
- 1 sporting goods store
- 9 women's and misses' apparel shops

1947

Advertisements on this page and the following page are from a 1947 edition of The Sentinel that was discovered in a wall in an old home that was being torn down. The old edition is owned by Randy Cutshall, of Lewistown.

1947

1959

1963

1963

1963

1962

1970

1970

1982

1990

1982

1999

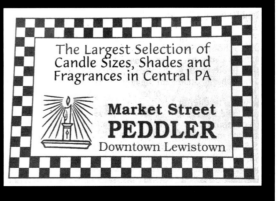

Page One

From the days of the first newspapers in the Juniata Valley until about 1970, the bottom half of the front page featured tiny advertisements of all sorts — from business specials to help wanted to special notices. These popular snippets are still remembered fondly by readers. Enjoy these examples on this page and the next two pages.

1916

WANTED

Experienced axe workmen for steel fitter and wheeler. Apply Mann Edge Tool Company..

PRAYER MEETINGS FOR APRIL 6

First ward: Mrs. Gussard, Stone Road, 1:30 p. m.

Third ward: Mrs. Jos. L. McKinney, North Brown street, 9 a. m.

Sixth ward: Mrs. Wm. Youtzy, 366 South Main street, 9 a. m.

FRANCIS X. BUSHMAN, TEMPLE TONIGHT, 6 O'CLOCK.

NOTICE

The Name Social which was to be given by the Daughters of Veterans tomorrow evening was postponed until April 27, 1916. Our regular meeting will be held tomorrow evening.

SPECIAL

Chicken and Waffle Supper From 5 to 7 p. m. Thursday, at Crystal Cafe. Price 50 cents.

Every Methodist should be at prayer service tonight, 7:30 o'clock.

EXPERT SEWING MACHINE REPAIRING

We have secured a factory experienced expert repairman for a few weeks only. Orders left for repairing and cleaning any make of machine will be promptly attended to at reasonable prices. Bratton's Music Store. Both phones.

Moving Pictures at the Milroy Rink Wednesday, Friday and Saturday evenings.

LET RUSS MEND YOUR SHOES

If it harrows your soul to have your soles wear out so soon let Ralph Russ do your shoe repairing and see how much longer your soles wear. We use a thoroughly high grade leather of unusual merit. I now have four expert helpers and am prepared to do all kinds of work expertly, turning over a neat job on the very day it is brought to my shop. No rush is too great for our corps of workers and latest machinery to handle satisfactorily.

Ralph Russ, 7 N. Main street.

1919

FOUR DAY SALE OF GOOD DRESSES CHEAP

We have just received a shipment of Sample Dresses in Spring Models of Taffeta, Assorted Styles and Shades. Special Prices $8.75 to $11.75. A saving of $2.00 to $5.00 on a Dress.

All Winter Coats in the sale will go reduced ¼ to 1-3 off Regular Prices.

FLISHER & RENALDS
27th, 28th, 29th 30th

KNIGHTS OF COLUMBUS

Will meet tomorrow evening, the 28th at 8 o'clock. Yours for a good turnout. S. V. Hassett, Grand Knight

1945

Wednesday A. M.
At The Princess Shop!
Final Clean-up Sale!
250 Dresses!
Lot No. 1 ....$2.00
Lot No. 2 ....$3.00
Lot No. 3 ....$4.00
Values to $8.95. Come early.
The Princess Shop.

Help wanted—Men-Women
Salespeople, steady work. No phone calls. Apply Rubin's, 12 E. Market St.

Restaurant For Sale
Stock, equipment and fixtures. Give reference in first letter. Good lease, reasonable rent. Write Box 198, c-o Sentinel.

Festival tonight at Juniata Terrace Playground. Concert by Burnham Band.

We pay top cash prices for used cars. Any make or model. Cupp Motor Company.

Eugene, Frederick, Truart, Empress, Violet Oil and Cold Waves greatly reduced for one week only. Dial 4182. Elizabeth Beauty Shop, 16 W. Market St.

Notice
Effective Monday, August 27, 1945 and until the sugar situation is relieved no ice cream will be sold through our dairy store to be carried out.
The only ice cream for sale will be for table service only.
Royale Dairy Company.

Everybody welcome to our parties on Monday and Wednesday evening at 8 o'clock, in the K. of C. Home, second floor, Novak's Garage, West Third Street.

1945

1961

coffee between 10 p.m. Sunday night and 7 a.m. Monday morning. The restaurant operator, Howard Johnson's Co., will underwrite the costs.

New Store Hours
Mon. thru Thurs. ....6-9 p.m.
Friday ....6-10 p.m.
Saturday ....9 a.m.-5 p.m.
Happy New Year
Rowe Gun & Machine Shops, Yeagertown.

Archery Shoot
Sunday, Dec. 31, at 1:30 p.m., at Seven Mountain Archery Club ground, Lingle Valley. Everybody welcome.

Capital Finance Corporation
Money for left over Christmas bills. 53 Valley St., 248-7827.

Milroy American Legion
Gala New Year's Eve party Dec. 31. Novelties and refreshments. Music by the Vicounts. Members and guests.

Tonight Come To Angelo's
For the dinner that is different. Lasagna, manicotti, Italian steak, chicken cacciatori, chops, etc. Also for the finest pizza anywhere. It's worth the drive of less than a mile on the Granville road. Phone 248-9502.

Brooklyn Members
New Year's Eve party. Dance to Harold Wilt's Orchestra. Novelties, noisemakers.

F. W. Black Hospital Aux.
Regular meeting postponed until Monday, Jan. 8.

Special—Pre New Year's Eve party Saturday evening, 10 till 2. Harold Wilt's Orchestra, noisemakers and hats for all. Welcome Inn, Reedsville.

West Granville Fire Co.
Square dance Saturday, 8:30 p.m. Jimmy Treaster, caller.

Fame Members
Dance to the Triads Saturday night, 10 till ?.

Sauerkraut supper at McVeytown Methodist Church Monday, Jan. 1, 4:30-7 p.m. Price: Adults $1.00, children 50c.

Eagle Members
Round and square dancing Sunday.

New Year's Eve Bowling
Starting at 11 o'clock enjoy moonlight bowling at the Lewistown Bowling Center on S. Main St. Watch for the red pin.

1962

learned.

sincere
at the
y physi-
e Fame
to my
es, and
it cards
prayed
stay in

Lepley.

es
.00.
:et.

r sale.

re
ncl.

l and
and

S&H Green Stamps
Free on all gas and oil sales.
Ike & Sons Cities Service Gas
Station, Open Hearth, Burnham.

Official Inspection Station
Shearer's Atlantic, Market and
Grand streets.

Airport Restaurant
Route 322, near Milroy. Now
open Thurs., Fri., Sat., and Sun.

Dr. M. Solomon DDS
Announces his association with
Dr. George Hoagland, 112 E. Mar-
ket St.

Park Ave. Beauty Salon
Closed for vacation July 9 to 23.

July Sales
Dresses, val. to $25, $8.95 to $17.95
$4 lingerie, odd lots $2.99
$6 lingerie, odd lots $3.99
Lila Ford.

Laugh a Day
Teacher (to little girl learning to
write)—"But where is the dot over
the i?"
"It's in the pencil yet!"

Thank You
To everyone who helped and
patronized our street fair and
circus.
Lewistown Lions Club.

Barrels For Sale
Get your cider barrels while
available. Beaver Bros. Baking
Co., Burnham.

Home Grown Tomatoes
4 lbs. $1.00.
Al & Jim's Fruit Basket.

'60 Moretti Sports Car
Convertible, white with black
top. Across from post office,
Belleville.

county committe
pected them late
Prolonged dry
plagued Pennsylv
more than nine s

Turkey
Sponsored by
istration Comm
July 12 at 6:30
Methodist Churc
ets $2.50 per pe:
the door.

Mingo Club me
gan H. S. Thurs
p.m. Election

Inspect
At Van's Che
S. Main St.

White's
Closed for vac:

Frigidaire Qu
We must sell
more at Fossel

1963

l'noon
lent's
Strings.

fices,
'pro-
losed
eral.
ores
un-
ma-

sug-
be
that
lual
id.
ted
t s
sed
the
a
on.
id-
fic
ite

Elks Club
Social scheduled for Monday has
been canceled.

Ronald E. Gilliland, Jeweler
Watches
17 jewels $11.95
21 jewels $14.95
Lay-away today. 4 Elm St.

Pizza—Chinese
Only at Angelo's, 248-9502.

Yeagertown Fire Co.
Dancing to The Playboys Saturday night, 10:30 to ?.

Space Diner
Sunday special, filled chopped
sirloin.

Peachey's Meats
Route 76, between Reedsville
and Belleville. Phone 667-2576. We
do custom butchering of all kinds
of meat and fowl.

Visit the new pumpkin bar at
Hotel Lewistown Dining Room.
Breakfast, lunch and dinner.

Ben Mar Tonigh
Back by popular deman
and the Impressions'' fi
York City.

Miller's Greenhou
Watch for our Tha
centerpiece special.

Square Dance
McClure Fire House,
son, caller.

Milroy American L
Post 287 serving Sunda
Nov. 24 from 12 till ?.
and roast turkey.

Milroy Alumni A
Dance scheduled for
Green Gables has been

East Derry Fire
Orchestra Sat. night
dancing, 10 till ?.

Converse All St
Basketball shoes, hi
cut, black or white,
team price $7.95.
Aurand's, 229 E.